C O N T E N T S

		Page
INTRODUCTION		1
1	**THE NEW CATEGORIES OF SCHOOL**	**3**
	Community schools	3
	Foundation schools	3
	Voluntary-aided schools	3
	Voluntary-controlled schools	4
	Special schools	4
	School names	4
2	**THE NEW CONSTITUTIONS OF GOVERNING BODIES**	**5**
	Community schools	5
	Foundation schools	5
	Voluntary-aided schools	6
	Voluntary-controlled schools	6
3	**THE CATEGORIES OF GOVERNOR**	**6**
	Parent governors	6
	Teacher governors	7
	Staff governors	7
	LEA governors	7
	Foundation governors	7
	Partnership governors	8
	Co-opted governors	8
	Additional co-opted governors	8
	Representative governors	9
	The headteacher	9
	The involvement of pupils	9
4	**ELIGIBILITY AND DISQUALIFICATIONS**	**10**
	Disqualifications	10
	Eligibility to serve	10
	Co-opted governors	10
	Partnership governors	11
	Appointed parent governors	11
	Teacher governors	11
	Deputy headteachers	11
	Headteachers	12
	Headteachers as teacher/parent governors	13
	Teacher governors becoming acting heads	13
	Employees as governors in other capacities	14
	Employees as parent governors at their own school	15
	Eligibility to chair meetings	15
	'Political' restrictions	15

5 TERMS OF OFFICE AND ELECTIONS   **16**

Terms of office   16
Elections   17
Review of governor numbers   19

6 THE ELECTED GOVERNOR'S POSITION   **19**

Controversial issues   20
Union representatives as elected governors   20
Employee governors: reconciling differences   21

7 THE REMOVAL OF GOVERNORS   **22**

Statutory disqualification   22
Elected governors   22
Appointed governors   23
Co-opted governors   24
Further proposals on removal   25
Removal of the chair   26
The clerk to the governors   26

8 GOVERNORS' RIGHTS AND LIABILITIES   **27**

The governors' constitutional position   27
   Governors visiting classrooms   27
   Governors' codes of practice   28
Allowances   28
Time off   29
Training for governors   29
Personal liability   29
Insurance   30
Criminal liability   30
The 'Nolan principles'   30
Register of Interests   31

9 PROCEEDINGS OF GOVERNING BODIES   **31**

The position of chair   32
Convening meetings – agendas and notice   33
Adjournments   33
Quorum   34
Taking decisions   34
Rescinding resolutions   34
Public access to meetings   34
Publication of agendas, minutes etc   34
Confidential issues   35

10 GOVERNORS' COMMITTEES AND RULES ON DELEGATION   **37**

Delegation of powers   37
   Restrictions on delegation   37
   'Compulsory' delegation to committees   38
   Delegation to a committee only   38
The operation of committees   39
Membership of committees   39

11 APPOINTING STAFF   **40**

Headteacher and deputy appointments   40
Other teacher appointments   41
Non-teaching staff appointments   42

12 DISCIPLINE AND DISMISSAL OF STAFF   **42**

Dismissal   42
   Community and voluntary-controlled schools   43
   Foundation and voluntary-aided schools   43
   The involvement of employee governors   44

13 POWERS OF INTERVENTION   **44**

LEA powers   44
The Code of Practice on LEA-School Relations   44
   Formal warning notice   45
   Appointing additional governors   45
   Suspending the delegated budget   45
   Breakdown of discipline   46
The Secretary of State's powers   47
   Appointing additional governors   47
   Directing closure   47
The diocesan authorities' powers   47

14 CONFLICTS OF INTEREST – WITHDRAWALS   **48**

Conflicts of interest   49
Ability to act impartially in hearings   50
Appointment panels   51

15 SIGNIFICANT CASE LAW   **52**

The removal of governors   52
   The independence of appointed governors   52
   Removals for 'political balance'   53
   'Natural justice' in removing governors   53
Pecuniary interest   53
   The appointment of staff   53
   Proposals for schools to change status   54
The appointment of staff   55
The dismissal of staff   56
Employers' right to refuse permission to employees to serve as governors   56

16 USEFUL FURTHER READING   **57**

17 HELPFUL ORGANISATIONS   **58**

APPENDIX A: THE NEW CONSTITUTIONS OF GOVERNING BODIES   59

Community schools   59
Foundation schools   60
Voluntary-aided schools   61
Voluntary-controlled schools   62
Special schools   63
Foundation special schools   64

APPENDIX B: THE EDUCATION (SCHOOL GOVERNMENT) (ENGLAND) REGULATIONS 1999   65

APPENDIX C: THE RECOMMENDATIONS OF THE HOUSE OF COMMONS EDUCATION AND EMPLOYMENT COMMITTEE INQUIRY REPORT: THE ROLE OF SCHOOL GOVERNORS, JULY 1999   99

INTRODUCTION

In September 1999, the Government completed the implementation of its major restructuring of maintained schools. The reforms of school governance introduced by the School Standards and Framework Act 1998 comprised three key elements:

■ firstly, in April 1999, the establishment of a **common funding system** for all state schools under the Fair Funding system. The Funding Agency for Schools (FAS), which was formerly responsible for funding grant-maintained (GM) schools, was abolished. Accordingly, all maintained schools are now funded directly by their maintaining local education authority (LEA) on a comparable basis under its local management scheme;

■ then, with effect from September 1999, the **restructuring** of maintained schools. This was achieved firstly by **redesignating** the five previous types of state schools (county, grant-maintained, voluntary-aided, voluntary-controlled and special-agreement) into four new categories: **community, foundation, voluntary-aided** (VA) and **voluntary-controlled** (VC) schools. The former **grant-maintained** (GM) category ceased to exist, as did **special-agreement** schools. Special schools continue, adopting one of the new categories. The new categories of school are described in Chapter 1.

At the same time (ie September 1999), the **composition** of governing bodies was substantially altered. The new constitutions provide for more parent governors, a new category of 'staff governor' and several other significant amendments. Chapter 2 and **Appendix A** set out the new constitutions in detail;

■ finally, also from September 1999, the rules on **school government** have been significantly amended. The **1999 School Government Regulations** adjust the rules as to how governing bodies operate, affecting in particular: delegations, voting rights, disqualifications, exclusions of governors and governors' removal from office. From now on, schools will have Instruments of Government, setting out their structure and constitution – but they will no longer have Articles of Government. The provisions formerly contained in the Articles will be subsumed into other legislation. The second part of this guide (and especially Chapters 9 and 10) explores these issues, and the Regulations themselves are reproduced as **Appendix B.**

Meanwhile, during the early Summer of 1999, the **House of Commons Education and Employment Committee** undertook an **inquiry** into the role of school governors. It reported in July 1999. The Committee's summary of its conclusions and recommendations is reproduced as **Appendix C,** and the findings and recommendations are also referred to at relevant places in the text.

This publication replaces the 1994 ATL handbook **The School Governor.** It explains the new categories of school, the types, position and responsibilities of school governors and – in particular – analyses the operation and proceedings of governing bodies. It attempts to offer concise but detailed guidance and advice – primarily for teacher, staff and parent governors – on the many challenging and sensitive issues which governors face.

These include the new rules on the appointment and dismissal of staff, and the powers of the LEA (and the Secretary of State) to intervene in governors' decisions. It sets out the legislation as at September 1999, but (needless to say) is not intended to offer a definitive or comprehensive explanation of the law.

This booklet is not intended to cover the position of governors in schools in **Northern Ireland** or in **colleges of further education,** which operate under their own Instruments of Government. Nevertheless, the general principles which underpin this guidance apply in both these cases also. Similarly, this publication is not addressed to **independent schools,** which are not governed by the legislation on school governance. Indeed, following the devolution of education matters to the **Welsh Assembly** it is possible that, in due course, different rules may apply to maintained schools in Wales.

Throughout this publication, the 1996 Education Act will be referred to as 'the 1996 Act', the 1998 School Standards and Framework Act as the 'SSFA 1998', local education authorities as 'LEAs', voluntary-aided schools as 'VA schools', and voluntary-controlled schools as 'VC schools'.

For ease of reference, the **1999 Education (School Government) (England) Regulations** are reproduced in full as Appendix B. Throughout this guide, they are referred to as 'the **1999 Regulations**'.

ATL is grateful to the DfEE (and particularly its School Framework and Governance Division) for information and helpful comments on the preparation of this booklet.

1 THE NEW CATEGORIES OF SCHOOL

From 1 September 1999, all maintained schools enter new legal categories. Their brief characteristics are as follows:

COMMUNITY SCHOOLS

These replace the previous **county** schools. The local authority owns the land and buildings and is the ultimate **employer** of the staff (although, under the established local management system, the governors retain most employment powers).

Schedule 16 of the SSFA 1998 continues – with some minor modifications – the existing rules as to the **appointment and dismissal** of staff by the governors, such as employees' rights to hearing and appeals (see Chapters 11 and 12). There are relatively minor changes to the former composition of the governing body (see Chapter 2).

In community schools, the LEA controls the dates of terms and holidays and the governing body decides the times of school sessions.

FOUNDATION SCHOOLS

These replace most former **grant-maintained** schools. They acquire two new **LEA governors** and are now funded direct from the local authority. The balance of representation on the governing body has shifted away from first/foundation governors towards parental representatives (see Chapter 2). Furthermore, new requirements – comparable to those in county/community schools – apply as to the **appointment and dismissal of staff** by the governing bodies of foundation

schools (see Chapter 12).

The governors may give advisory rights to the LEA on appointments and dismissals. However, there is also considerable continuity: the **governing body remains the employer** of the staff – and (as before) controls both the dates of school terms and holidays, and the times of school sessions.

The school premises are either held on trust by a foundation (or a specially-constituted 'foundation body') or held by the governing body itself.

Foundation schools are 'exempt charities' (ie they have charitable status but are not subject to the jurisdiction of the Charity Commission and cannot formally register as charities).

VOLUNTARY-AIDED SCHOOLS

The present voluntary-aided category (essentially for church schools) has been preserved. Existing VA schools, and GM schools which were formerly VA, have generally adopted this category, as have special-agreement schools.

As before, the **governing body remains the employer** and is required to fund (normally via its church provider) 15 per cent of capital projects. The school governors continue to decide both the dates of school terms and holidays and the school session times. The school premises are normally held on trust by a foundation or by the governors themselves. Like foundation schools, VA schools are 'exempt charities' (see above).

The two significant alterations here – from September 1999 – are the changes to the composition of the governing body (see Chapter 2) and, in common with foundation schools, the introduction of statutory rules over the **appointment and dismissal of staff** under the SSFA 1998 (see Chapters 11 and 12).

VOLUNTARY-CONTROLLED SCHOOLS

This existing category has also been retained in the new structure (although this was in doubt until late into the consultation prior to the SSFA 1998).

Again, the previous status quo has been largely retained: the LEA employs the staff, and the schools retain their religious ethos via a church/foundation which holds the premises on trust and has the right to appoint foundation governors. Like foundation schools, VC schools are 'exempt charities' (see above).

In these schools, the only key change – from September 1999 – is the adjustment of the constitution of the governing body (see Chapter 2).

SPECIAL SCHOOLS

The indicative categories for **special schools** in the new structure are either 'community-special' (for former maintained special schools) or 'foundation-special' (for former GM special schools).

Virtually all maintained schools have transferred to their 'indicative' category, as above. However, there has been a procedure under which the governing bodies of former GM schools can opt (in some cases, following a parental ballot) for a different new category. A **Times** **Educational Supplement** survey in the Spring of 1999 found that only eight of the 1,200 former GM schools had in fact chosen to 'return to the LEA fold' as community schools, rather than moving to their indicative category of foundation or VA schools.

SCHOOL NAMES

Some schools have needed a **name change** to ensure that their name is not misleading and does not refer to an obsolete category (eg '...grant-maintained' or 'special-agreement' school). However, the DfEE has been tolerant of the retention of **existing** names, such as '... grammar school' even if the school is not wholly selective, or '...community school' even though the school will not now be in this specific category. Choosing a name for a school is stated in DfEE Circular 15/98 **New Framework Governing Bodies** to be essentially a matter for the governing body rather than for the LEA – although consultation is, of course, encouraged.

2 THE NEW CONSTITUTIONS OF GOVERNING BODIES

By 1 September 1999, each maintained school should have been redesignated as a community, foundation, voluntary-aided or voluntary-controlled school and should have:

■ **adopted** a new constitution as to its governor composition (making a **choice** of composition where provided for), and

■ **reconstituted** the membership of its governing body in accordance with the new constitution, ensuring appointments and removals as required.

The exception to this rule is that grouped schools are not required to set up separate governing bodies until 31 December 1999. **DfEE Circular 15/98 New Framework Governing Bodies** – and the Education (School Government – Transition to New Framework) Regulations 1998, SI 1998 No 2763 – provide the details of these requirements. The main changes from the previous structure are that:

■ many schools (particularly primaries) get **more choice** as to the size and composition of the governing body;

■ virtually all schools have more **parent governors;**

■ new **staff governors** (representing the non-teaching staff) are introduced in all but the smallest schools;

■ foundation (formerly GM) schools acquire two new LEA governors while losing some first/foundation governors.

The total membership of the governing body has increased in many schools.

Appendix A sets out the new constitutions (and their comparison with the previous compositions) for each category of school. However, the main adjustments for each type, from September 1999, are as follows:

COMMUNITY SCHOOLS

■ Most acquire at least **one parent governor;**

■ they acquire a new (non-teaching) **staff governor** – unless, in the case of primaries with under 100 pupils, they have opted not to;

■ most have fewer **co-opted** places;

■ all secondaries now have **two teacher governors** (some smaller secondary schools previously had only one);

■ in **primaries,** some have opted for a model with **two teacher governors** where there was formerly only one. Others may have chosen a 'smaller' model – even, in some cases, reducing from two teacher governors to one.

FOUNDATION SCHOOLS

■ Many acquire one or two **more parent governors;**

■ they acquire a new (non-teaching) **staff governor** – unless, in the case of schools with under 100 pupils, they have opted not to;

■ all acquire two new **LEA governors;**

■ all now have fewer **foundation (or partnership) governors** than they previously had first governors. As a result, the balance of power on the governing body has changed;

■ all acquire **co-opted governor(s)** (GM schools previously had none);

■ all **secondaries** now have **two teacher governors** (some secondary GM schools had only one);

■ **primaries** now have only one teacher governor (some GM schools previously had two).

VOLUNTARY-AIDED (VA) SCHOOLS

■ The previous wide flexibility which enabled VA schools to set their own constitutions within broad limits has been replaced by more **rigid options;**

■ many secondaries and some primaries acquire at least **one more parent governor;**

■ they acquire a new (non-teaching) **staff governor** – unless, in the case of

primaries with under 100 pupils, they have opted not to;

■ all **secondaries** now have **two teacher governors** (some smaller schools previously had only one);

■ **primaries** now have only **one teacher governor** (some VA schools previously had two).

VOLUNTARY-CONTROLLED (VC) SCHOOLS

■ Most acquire at least **one more parent governor;**

■ they acquire a new (non-teaching) **staff governor** – unless, in the case of primaries with under 100 pupils, they have opted not to;

■ in the largest primaries, some VC schools may now have only one teacher governor where they previously had two.

3 THE CATEGORIES OF GOVERNOR

PARENT GOVERNORS

Parent governors are parents of registered pupils at the school. They are **elected by parents** by secret ballot. Questions as to who is a parent, for the purposes of standing as a parent governor or for voting in elections, are a matter for the LEA in the case of community and VC schools, and for the governing body in the case of foundation and VA schools. However, in accordance with the principles of the Children Act 1989, it appears that all those with 'parental responsibility' for a pupil (including

separated or divorced parents, and guardians) are entitled to vote.

Parent governors hold office for four years and may then be re-elected if they are still eligible as parents. If, however, their child leaves the school during their period of office, parent governors are not obliged to resign before completing the four-year term. Similarly, they cannot be removed by the parents they represent.

Where insufficient numbers of parents stand for election, the governing body has the power to **appoint parent governors** without election. This power to appoint parent governors similarly arises in a maintained school where 50 per cent or more of the pupils are **boarders** and it appears impracticable to hold an election. The appointee(s) should be either a parent of a pupil at the school or (if this is not reasonably practicable) a person who is the parent of a child of compulsory school age – see also page 11 (Schedule 2 of the 1999 Regulations). In the case of special schools not established in a hospital, there are further requirements as to appointees.

From June 2000, the parent governors of each LEA are entitled to elect between two and five **parent governor representatives** on the authority's education committee(s) (The Education (Parent Governor Representatives) Regulations 1999, SI 1999, No 1949).

TEACHER GOVERNORS

Teacher governors are elected by the **teachers** at the school from among their number by secret ballot. Their term of office is four years, but it terminates automatically if they leave the school's employment in the interim, creating a vacancy to be filled by election. For community and VC schools, the local authority has the power to determine who is 'a teacher at the school' under Schedule 4 of the 1999 Regulations. In the case of foundation and VA schools, the decision is the responsibility of the governing body (these issues are explored in more detail in 'Eligibility to Serve' on page 10). Teacher governors cannot be removed by their colleagues.

STAFF GOVERNORS

These are a new category of governor created by the SSFA 1998 to take office from September 1999. All maintained schools, except small primaries who adopt the smallest constitution (see Appendix A), will now have staff governors. They are elected by – and drawn from – the **non-teaching staff** at the school for a four year term by secret ballot. In common with teacher governors, their position is terminated if they leave the school's employment. Again, they cannot be removed by their colleagues.

LEA GOVERNORS

LEA governors are appointed by the local authority to serve for a term of four years, and can be re-appointed. They are frequently chosen to reflect the interests of political parties. In principle, LEA governors can be removed by the authority at any time, but see Chapter 7 for detailed information on this issue.

FOUNDATION GOVERNORS

These governors hold office in VA, VC and many foundation schools. They are appointed by the body (or bodies) named in the school's Instrument of Government (normally a church authority or voluntary organisation) to represent that body's interests. Some hold office *ex officio*. Foundation governors who are not members *ex officio* normally serve for four years, but those appointed on or after 1 September 1999 may be given shorter terms of office.

In VA schools, a certain number of foundation governors must be parents of pupils at the school: three in larger secondaries and two in other cases (see Appendix A).

In principle, foundation governors can be removed from office by the appointing body at any time but, again, see Chapter 7 for a detailed explanation. Foundation governors can be re-appointed for a further term.

If an *ex officio* foundation governor is unable or unwilling to act as a governor (or there is a vacancy in the *ex officio* position in question), the appointing body is entitled to appoint a **substitute governor** to undertake the role in the meantime (Regulation 8 of the 1999 Regulations). See also page 17 for the substitute governor's term of office.

PARTNERSHIP GOVERNORS

Partnership governors exist only at foundation schools which do not have a foundation or trustees (generally former county GM schools). In these circumstances, they take the place of foundation governors and are appointed by the other governors. The governing body must seek nominations of those who are members of the community served by the school and who are 'committed to its good government and success' (Schedule 3 of the 1999 Regulations). Their term of office is also four years.

When nominations for partnership governors are required, they must be invited from parents. Existing governors are not entitled to nominate candidates for partnership governors – unless there are insufficient nominees (Schedule 3 of

the 1999 Regulations).

Certain groups are ineligible to be partnership governors: parents of pupils at the school, its employees and members and employees of the maintaining LEA (Schedule 5 of the 1999 Regulations).

CO-OPTED GOVERNORS

These governors are appointed by the other (non-co-opted) members of the governing body for the customary four-year term. All school categories, except VA schools, include co-opted governors in their constitutions. The intention is to enable the school to introduce specific areas of expertise. The long-established expectation is that the co-optees will include members of the community served by the school (including the local business community), but this does not appear as a requirement in the 1999 Regulations.

Again, certain groups are **ineligible** to be co-opted: employees at the school, its pupils (even if aged over 18) and elected members of the maintaining LEA. However, unlike partnership governors, LEA employees can be appointed as co-optees, as can parents (Schedule 6 of the 1999 Regulations).

The 1999 School Government Regulations introduce a new procedure for the governing body to **remove** co-opted governors (see Chapter 7).

ADDITIONAL CO-OPTED GOVERNORS

In certain circumstances, the governing body is either required or entitled to appoint additional co-optees (Schedule 1 of the 1999 Regulations). A community,

VA or VC **primary** school in an area serving a minor authority (a parish community or district council) is **required** to appoint an additional co-opted governor nominated by the authority. In the case of a school with a **sponsor** (ie a person or body who voluntarily gives substantial financial assistance to the school) or a school in an **education action zone,** the sponsor – or the Education Action Forum, as appropriate – **may** be invited to nominate an additional co-optee (see Appendix A.)

REPRESENTATIVE GOVERNORS

These are appointed only at community special schools. They are **obligatory** in such schools established in a hospital. Where the school is not established in a hospital, the LEA **may** designate a voluntary organisation to appoint a representative governor.

THE HEADTEACHER

Headteachers may choose whether or not to be a governor, and may change their mind on the issue by notifying the clerk to governors in writing. The initial assumption is that headteachers will act as governors, since they must inform the clerk if they do **not** intend to be governors (Regulation 17 of the 1999 Regulations).

If the head elects not to be a governor, s/he is nevertheless entitled to attend meetings of the governing body and its committees (Regulations 32 and 56).

THE INVOLVEMENT OF PUPILS

There is no category of 'pupil governor'. Indeed, the School Government Regulations make it exceedingly difficult for pupils to be directly involved in school governance by disqualifying any person **under 18 years** of age from becoming a governor. Furthermore, pupils at the school cannot be chosen as **co-opted governors** (Schedule 6 of the 1999 Regulations). It is possible, therefor, for (adult) pupils to be governors (in the appointed category, for example), but in ATL's experience this is rare.

The inquiry on **The Role of the School Governor** published by the House of Commons Education and Employment Committee in July 1999 considered the absence of pupil involvement to be a mistake (see Appendix C). It recommends the establishment of consultative arrangements such as School Councils. Paragraph 51 of the report concludes as follows:

'We have therefor considered other ways in which pupils' views can be taken into account. Many schools have a School Council – a representative body comprised of pupils, elected by the pupil body. We noted the value of such councils in our 1998 report on disaffected children, and commented that they could help pupils learn citizenship skills – a point also made at our informal meeting in Leeds.

'**We welcome the existence of School Councils, and wish to see all schools establish such bodies. We recommend that governing bodies establish consultative arrangements to ensure governors are aware of pupils' opinions. Such arrangements should include opportunities for pupils to make presentations to the governing body, or for a governor to attend, by invitation, meetings of the School Council.** Where School Councils do not exist, we recommend that governing bodies consider other means of consulting pupils'.

4 ELIGIBILITY AND DISQUALIFICATIONS

The new Education (School Government) (England) Regulations 1999 revise and expand the previous rules both as to **eligibility** to serve as a school governor and to **disqualifications** from governorship or from certain roles on the governing body. The Regulations are reproduced in full in Appendix B and are referred to here as 'the 1999 Regulations'.

DISQUALIFICATIONS

Schedule 6 of the 1999 Regulations confirms the existing categories of disqualifications and introduces some additions and refinements. The main long-established disqualifications apply to those who:

■ have been convicted of a serious **criminal offence** and been sentenced to three months or more imprisonment (or, in the case of a conviction for causing a nuisance or disturbance as a trespasser on school premises, a fine) in the last five years;

■ are **under** 18 years of age;

■ are adjudged **bankrupt** (and have not been discharged);

■ already hold the **maximum** number of **two governorships** (disregarding the permitted maximum of two *ex officio* governorships);

■ are governors, but have **failed to attend** meetings without consent for six months. (This rule does not apply to *ex officio* governors.) The 1999 Regulations add that, when a governor sends in apologies for a meeting, the minutes should now record whether the governing body consents to the absence (a copy of the minutes is to be sent to the governor in question). Further, the Regulations preclude further re-appointment during the 12 months following disqualification.

The 1999 Regulations also confirm that a person cannot hold governorships in **more than one category** (eg teacher governor and parent governor) in the same school at the same time.

The **further** disqualifications (from September 1999) affect those who:

■ are 'sectioned' (liable to be detained) under the **Mental Health Act**;

■ have been **disqualified** from serving as a **company director** (or are subject to an order under the Insolvency Act);

■ have been **removed as charity trustees** by the Charity Commissioners or the Court;

■ are **named in 'List 99'** (the Secretary of State's list of barred or restricted teachers and other workers with children and young persons);

■ are disqualified from being the **proprietor (or an employee) of an independent school** by an order under the 1996 Act.

ELIGIBILITY TO SERVE

The 1999 Regulations introduce some significant restrictions as to who may serve in certain categories:

Co-opted governors

Co-opted governors cannot now be appointed from pupils or employees at the school, nor from elected members of the LEA.

Partnership governors

Partnership governors (who take the place of foundation governors in foundation schools without trustees or a foundation – see page 8) cannot be chosen from parents, pupils, or employees at the school, nor from elected members or employees of the LEA.

Appointed parent governors

Appointed parent governors (ie those selected by the governing body when there are insufficient nominees – see page 6) cannot be chosen from employees of the LEA or its maintained schools, nor from elected members of the LEA – unless they are also a parent of a pupil at the school.

Teacher governors

To serve as a teacher governor, a candidate must be a teacher at the school. It is the **LEA** in the case of community and VC schools, and the **governing body** in the case of foundation and VA schools, that decides who is eligible to serve as a teacher governor (Schedule 4 of the 1999 Regulations). The SSFA 1998 (Schedule 9) makes clear that the teachers eligible both to vote and to stand for election include not only employees but also those 'otherwise engaged to provide services as a teacher'.

Clearly, the fact that a candidate works only **part-time** at the school does not invalidate her/his nomination. It can be argued that a part-time teacher who carries the confidence of colleagues may take a more detached view of staffroom controversy, and may indeed have more time to devote to the increased responsibilities of being a teacher governor, than colleagues working longer hours. The election of part-timers to serve as teacher governors appears to be rare, however: most teachers seem to wish to be represented by full-time colleagues, perhaps judging them more likely to be conversant with the mood and views of the staff.

Similarly, there is nothing to prevent a candidate employed under a **temporary or fixed-term contract** from standing for election as a teacher governor. However, nominating for a four-year term of office a teacher who is confident of working at the school only for a limited period raises serious practical considerations. Such a candidate – and the teachers voting – may ask themselves whether it is wise to elect a teacher governor whose influence might not be strong. It would also be known that s/he would have to vacate the governor's place immediately upon leaving the staff of the school. There would seem to ATL very few cases in which it would make sense for such a teacher to be invited to stand, or to accept nomination.

In accordance with the definition above, **supply and peripatetic teachers** are also 'teachers at the school' and therefor eligible to stand for election (and to vote). However, similar issues of longevity in the school and capacity to fully represent colleagues appear to apply to their nomination.

Deputy headteachers

Notwithstanding obvious differences in their level of managerial responsibility and the different conditions of employment under which they work, deputy headteachers are not distinguished from other teachers in the legislation as far as teacher governorships are concerned. They are therefor **eligible** to serve as (and vote in the elections for) teacher governors. The Regulations do not, of course, permit deputy headteachers to deputise or 'substitute' for the headteacher as a governor when s/he is unable to attend a governing body meeting, but deputies may – in appropriate circumstances – serve as 'acting' headteacher governors (see page 13).

There is no legal reason why deputy headteachers should not stand for election as teacher governors. However, ATL suggests that deputies should consider the following issues.

The legislation provides for the headteacher and the teaching staff to be separately represented on governing bodies. The provision for both categories recognises that their views and interests will not always be identical: on occasions, indeed, they may differ sharply and the differences are a proper matter for a governing body to consider.

As a senior member of the teaching staff, whether or not formally designated a member of a senior management team, a deputy owes on-the-job loyalty to her/his head, either when carrying out policy decisions or when taking action on matters which affect the day-to-day running of the school. A deputy may not necessarily agree with these policies or their operational implications: nevertheless, it is her/his job to support them.

If elected as a teacher governor, however, the deputy head's role is to **present the views of the teaching staff** faithfully and reasonably. That duty is at

no time more important than when the teaching staff and the head do not take the same view.

Before being nominated, deputies should consider whether the managerial loyalty they owe to their headteacher can be reconciled with their duty to teacher colleagues, if the two come in conflict. Some will see no difficulty – and indeed the teacher constituency may elect deputy heads as teacher governors precisely **because** they want senior and respected members of staff to represent their views on the governing body, and trust the deputy head to take on this responsibility.

It would be quite wrong to exclude deputy heads from serving as teacher governors. If they do take on this role, however, they should recognise that they may face occasional and sometimes sharp conflicts of loyalty. They must be aware of this, and confident that they could deal with the situation sensitively.

HEADTEACHERS

The SSFA 1998 (Schedule 9) gives headteachers an *ex officio* place on the governing body, unless they decide not to take it. Where a head declines to serve as a governor, s/he nevertheless has the right to attend governing body meetings.

In practice, most heads will wish to participate as fully as possible in governing bodies' proceedings – particularly now that governors' powers are so extensive. Most therefor choose to serve as headteacher governors.

All the same, some may decide that their impartiality and professional commitment to carry out the governors' policies, whatever their personal opinion, are best demonstrated if they do **not** serve as governors but attend meetings as non-voting observers, available to provide professional advice when called upon to do so. Other heads may choose to serve as governors but to abstain from voting, particularly over major and/or controversial policy issues. These are quite respectable points of view.

Education legislation has traditionally defined 'headteacher' as including an **acting headteacher.** Therefor a teacher (normally the deputy) designated acting head while the actual head is absent from duty – or pending the appointment of a substantive head – is entitled to serve as a governor in the same way as a 'permanent' head. The permanent post-holder will resume these rights and responsibilities only when s/he returns to her/his duties as headteacher.

Designated headteachers of new schools yet to come into existence are entitled to serve as governors on temporary governing bodies or, if they decide not to do so, to attend all meetings of the governing body as an observer.

Headteachers as teacher/parent governors

Despite headteachers' entitlement to serve as *ex officio* governors, the legislation (perhaps oddly) does not specifically preclude them from serving as elected governors. It seems unlikely that the law-makers intended that heads should do this, but the Regulations' silence on the issue creates uncertainty.

A head cannot be an elected or appointed governor, and at the same time take up her/his *ex officio* place as headteacher, since one person cannot occupy two governorships simultaneously. However, a head could decline the *ex officio* governorship and stand for election as a teacher governor, or as a parent governor (if s/he has children at the school).

ATL suggests that it would be quite inappropriate for a headteacher to seek nomination as a governor in another capacity.

In the same way, ATL considers that the question of whether the head should exercise her/his **right to vote** in teacher or parent governor elections is problematic. Certainly s/he should studiously avoid nominating or promoting the election of any individual candidate, since (even in a secret ballot) the democratic nature of the election could be affected if it was thought a particular nominee had the head's backing. It would be wise for heads to avoid any suggestion that they are seeking to extend their influence in this way. For this reason, the Association also argues that it is normally preferable for the headteacher not to act as returning officer in a governor election.

Teacher governors becoming acting heads

If a teacher governor becomes acting head, s/he must choose whether to take up the *ex officio* place reserved for the head and resign as teacher governor, or to remain a teacher governor and decline the *ex officio* place for the 'acting headteacher' governor.

The acting head must, of course, be fully committed to the fulfilment of her/his new, albeit temporary, responsibilities. ATL therefor suggests that, for the reasons explained above, s/he should normally resign from the teacher governorship, thus creating a vacancy. An election can then be held so that the successful candidate can take up office as teacher governor as soon as possible (and preferably no later than when the acting head commences her/his new duties). The acting head then serves as the headteacher governor, and the professional view of the other teaching staff is separately represented – as the law clearly intends. ATL does not believe that it is desirable for an acting head who is a teacher governor to decline to act as headteacher governor while retaining her/his place as a teacher representative.

For all these reasons, ATL believes that neither headteachers nor acting heads should serve as elected teacher governors. On balance, the Association also considers that heads and acting heads should refrain from voting in teacher governor elections.

EMPLOYEES AS GOVERNORS IN OTHER CAPACITIES

The fact that a person is an employee at a school does not preclude her/him from holding a school governorship in certain other categories, eg as a parent governor or as a governor appointed by a local authority, either at her/his own school or at another school.

There has been controversy over this issue. Some observers argue that school staff should only serve as governors at schools at which they work if they are elected as teacher or staff governors by their colleagues. These observers suggest that employees who serve in any other capacity

reduce the lay involvement intended by the legislation, and increase the influence of the professional educational interest to a level which is undesirably dominant.

ATL disagrees, considering that **school employees should not be prevented from playing a full part in the life of the community merely by virtue of their occupation.** If a teacher/parent, for instance, is willing to serve on the governing body of the school attended by her/his child, and wins a majority of votes from other parents in a democratically-conducted (and secret) ballot, ATL sees no reason why that person should not take her/his place as **parent governor** (subject to the considerations below).

Nor does ATL see any reason why members of school staff should not play a positive role in local government. For example, a school secretary, either as a locally-active member of a political party, or as an elected member of a local authority, should be able to play a full part in the authority's affairs, including serving as an LEA appointee on school governing bodies (but see page 15 for guidance on some legal restrictions on this right).

However, the 1999 Regulations do introduce one **significant new restriction:** those eligible to be a teacher or staff governor are now **precluded from acting as co-opted governors at their own school.** They can serve as a co-opted governor at a different school.

Having said that, ATL offers the following comments and guidance for teachers contemplating standing for governorships in other capacities at their own school:

Employees as parent governors at their own school

An employee who works at the school attended by her/his child(ren) is entitled to stand and to be elected to serve as a **parent governor** of that school.

However, ATL cautions that s/he should think very carefully before doing so, and the following advice also has implications for a member of staff whose child attends the school where s/he works and who contemplates serving as a **teacher or staff governor**.

An employee in this position stands in a dual relationship to the school. As a member of staff, s/he has the opportunity to influence the governors' decision-making process by seeking election as a teacher or staff governor. S/he is also subject to the headteacher's day-to-day management, which is exercised within the policy framework decided by the governing body. As the parent of a child at the school, however, the employee is both a provider and, through the child, a recipient of the school's educational services.

ATL believes that an employee elected to be a parent governor at the school where s/he works could find problems in distinguishing between the two roles. It could be difficult for the member of staff (and also for the other governors) to know whether s/he was speaking primarily as an employee or as a parent on any given issue.

There would be the real possibility, too, that conflicts of interest could arise because the parent governor was also an employee. When this happened, and it became necessary for her/him to withdraw from a governors' meeting (see Chapter 14), s/he would obviously be unable to discharge the role of parent governor fully and in the way plainly intended by the legislation.

On balance, therefor, ATL considers that **an employee should not normally seek to serve as a parent governor at a school at which s/he works.** For many of the same reasons, a teacher who has children at her/his school should also think carefully about serving as a teacher governor.

ATL does **not**, however, think that the same considerations apply to a teacher or other employee **voting** in elections for parent governors when s/he has children at a school where s/he works. The ballot is secret, so that her/his personal preference can (and, in ATL's view, should) remain unknown: s/he has as much legal right as any other parent to be represented on the governing body, and there should be no attempt to curtail it.

ELIGIBILITY TO CHAIR MEETINGS

Teacher governors (and any other governors who may be employed at the school – including the headteacher) are **not** eligible for election as chair or vice-chair of the governing body. They are also ineligible to chair governors' committees (see Appendix B, regulations 27 and 43).

'POLITICAL' RESTRICTIONS

The Local Government Act 1972 prevents staff in schools maintained by an LEA (as well as other local authority employees) from holding office as a councillor in that authority.

The Local Government and Housing Act 1989 also places restrictions on certain local authority employees who occupy 'politically restricted' posts. **These do not include headteachers, principals, teachers or lecturers.**

The Act does, however, have implications for teachers and other staff who are **elected members of neighbouring local authorities,** because it provides that the interests of an authority in negotiations over the terms and conditions under which its staff are employed may not be represented by either:

■ anyone who is a **council member** and also in local authority **employment**; or

■ anyone who is a **council member** and also an official or employee of a **trade union** with members in local authority employment.

The Act therefor prevents a teacher who is employed by an authority and who is also an elected member of another authority from representing that other authority in negotiations with its employees over employment issues.

Additionally, union executive committee members, branch secretaries and even school representatives (ie any union office holders) who are also local council members could not represent **any** authority in these matters. There is no restriction on their participation on the **employees' side** in local or national negotiations: the prohibition applies only to their representing local authority interests.

Since **teacher and staff governors** are elected to represent their colleagues, not the LEA, the restrictions imposed by the Act do not apply to them in that role. However, employees who are elected members of local authorities and who serve on school governing bodies as **authority nominees** (ie LEA governors) are restricted from representing the interests of the authority in negotiations on pay, conditions or other matters affecting the employment of the authority's teacher or other employees. However, this would not, in ATL's view, preclude those governors from participating in discussions on a school's pay policy or the implementation of salary descriptions, since these are not 'negotiations'.

5   TERMS OF OFFICE AND ELECTIONS

TERMS OF OFFICE

The 1999 Regulations (see Appendix B) establish, from September 1999, a standard term of office of **four years** for most governors. This applies to parent, teacher, staff, LEA and co-opted governors (Regulation 16). However, in some circumstances, governors (mostly foundation governors) may serve for longer or shorter periods than the now customary four years. The main ones are as follows:

■ governors **continuing in office** on 1 September 1999 at the reconstitution of school governing bodies, hold office for the **remainder of their existing term** up to a maximum of four years (Schedule 7);

- **foundation** governors appointed on or after 1 September 1999 hold office for **up to four years,** their term being decided by the appointing body and notified at the time of appointment (Regulation 16 (1) (b));
- the **headteacher** has no limit on her/his tenure in office – effectively acting as an *ex officio* governor (Regulation 16 (1));
- a **co-opted** governor appointed to the **initial** constitution of a **new school** has a one-year term (Regulation 16 (1) (c));
- a **substitute governor** (ie a foundation governor appointed in place of an *ex officio* foundation governor who is unwilling or unable to act) holds office for four years **or** the return of the original governor **or** the arrival in the *ex officio* position of a new postholder – whichever is the sooner (Regulation 16 (2) and (3));
- **additional governors** nominated by the **Secretary of State** to schools requiring **special measures** are appointed for whatever term s/he decides (see Chapter 13). However, any additional governors appointed by the LEA or the appointing body to schools in difficulties are subject to the normal four-year term (Regulation 16 (1) (d)).

Needless to say, governors who reach the end of their term are eligible (subject to any rules on disqualification – see Chapter 4) to be re-elected or re-appointed.

ELECTIONS

Any contested election for a parent, teacher or staff governor must be held by **secret ballot.** The 1999 Regulations (see Appendix B, Schedule 4) provide that the arrangements for the election are controlled by the LEA (in the case of community and VC schools) or the governing body (for foundation and VA schools). However, the governors of a foundation or VA school may agree with the LEA that it will make the arrangements for them.

The authority or governors, as appropriate, may delegate most of these arrangements to the **headteacher**, but cannot delegate decisions as to whether or not a person is eligible to be a candidate or to vote in the election (ie whether they are to be considered a parent, teacher or member of the non-teaching staff). In elections for parent governors, the principles of the Children Act 1989 suggest that all those with parental responsibility for a pupil (which may include separated or divorced parents) are entitled to stand for election and to vote.

The Regulations impose only a minimum number of requirements as to elections:

- the LEA (or governors, as appropriate) may set **qualifying dates,** but cannot impose a minimum number of votes for a candidate to achieve in order to be elected;
- for **parent governor** elections, the voters are entitled to **vote by mail** or (if they prefer) by 'pupil post';
- for **parent governor** elections, reasonable steps must be taken to ensure that all eligible voters are **aware of the vacancy** and of their right to stand as a candidate and to vote, and that they are given an opportunity to do so (Schedule 4 of the 1999 Regulations).

The Regulations make **no specific provisions** on issues such as:

- who may **nominate** a governor. In the absence of rules being set by the LEA or governing body (as appropriate), it would appear that candidates may nominate themselves without a seconder;
- the **time limits** for **nominations** and **voting** – and whether these can be adjusted (eg to allow further time if nominations are sparse);
- the precise **mechanism of voting** (eg how the secrecy of the ballot will be secured);
- any arrangements for election 'manifestos' or **addresses** by the candidates.

All these are issues for the LEA or governing body to decide, according to the type of school, as outlined above. Objections to such decisions could be pursued through an appropriate grievance procedure or, in serious cases, through the Local Government Ombudsman. For example, in 1995, a parent governor in a Humberside school complained of maladministration to the Ombudsman after the LEA refused to intervene in a bungled election. Ballot papers for the parent governor vacancy had been distributed on a one-per-child (rather than one-per-parent) basis – resulting in nearly twice the correct number being issued. His complaint was upheld – although, in the event, the election was not re-run. Ultimately, it would be possible to invite the Secretary of State to intervene under Section 496 of the 1996 Act (unreasonable exercise of power by an LEA or governing body) or even to pursue a legal challenge in the High Court. However, instances are extremely rare.

Note that, where insufficient parent governors stand for election, the governing body has the power to **appoint parent governors** without an election (see pages 7 and 11 on eligibility).

ATL considers that the fairest method of conducting ballots where there is more than one candidate is by the **single transferable vote** (STV) system recommended by Electoral Reform Ballot Services. Accordingly, ATL recommends the use of the STV system in parent and teacher governor elections. A booklet offering a concise explanation of how this system operates is available free from Electoral Reform Ballot Services (see Chapter 17 for the address).

Headteachers are often nominated as returning officers in school governor elections. It may, however, be argued that this is not the best practice, since it would be undesirable for a head to be involved in any dispute over the conduct of the election. ATL suggests, therefor, that it is preferable for the LEA central or area administrator, or the clerk, as appropriate, to act as returning officer wherever possible.

In any event, ATL considers that **impartial scrutiny** of the election process should be possible, where necessary. Should there be a dispute over an election for which an LEA is responsible, ATL's view is that the Chief Education Officer should decide the matter. Where the governing body is responsible, ATL recommends referral to independent adjudication.

County and controlled schools are presently required, under Section 82 of the 1996 Act, to review the constitution of their governing bodies at least every four years, or more frequently if an event such as a transfer of site, or some other alteration, results in a change in pupil numbers.

If, after September 1999, it becomes necessary to **reduce** the number of governors in a particular category at any time as a result of a fall in the number of registered pupils at the school, and if the reduction cannot be achieved by voluntary resignations, the **governor with the shortest service** must relinquish her/his place. If such a distinction is not possible – because, for example, the governors were all elected to serve terms of office which started on the same date – then (under Regulation 13 of the 1999 regulations) lots should be drawn to decide who should stand down.

This system of arbitrary removals based on 'seniority' seems to ATL to be rough justice, which should be applied only as a last resort. There is nothing to prevent an alternative which ATL considers fairer, ie for all the teacher and/or parent governors concerned to agree to **resign** their posts so that **fresh elections** for a smaller number of vacancies may be held. The resigning governors may, of course, offer themselves as candidates.

6 THE ELECTED GOVERNOR'S POSITION

This chapter specifically concerns the role of governors elected to represent employees' or parents' interests. For these governors, a key question arises: **do elected governors serve in a representative or personal capacity?**

Parent, teacher and staff governors are, as a legal requirement, directly elected to the governing body. ATL believes that these governors must be free to exercise their own personal judgement over issues on which the governing body must take a decision. This means that these governors cannot be required by anyone to take a particular line on any matter, or to remain silent on an issue; nor can they be mandated to vote in a particular way or to abstain. To that extent, therefor, they serve in a personal capacity and – somewhat like Members of Parliament – parent, teacher and staff governors are **representatives rather than delegates**.

At the same time, they are elected – and that implies an expectation (on the part of teachers, non-teaching staff, parents and the governing body itself) that they will faithfully voice the views of their 'constituents'.

ATL therefor believes that elected governors are under a clear duty to register the views of the group they represent, even when their personal opinion may be different.

CONTROVERSIAL ISSUES

Some governing bodies will want to (or will have to) consider issues of real controversy, on which opinions within the governing body, among employees and parents, and in the wider public arena, will be sharply – even bitterly – divided. How should elected governors behave in such circumstances?

The opinions of the employees or parents represented by a governor may well be split. Their views may also be subject to change as the debate progresses. Union representatives may forcefully express opinions which are not necessarily shared by all members of their association or by the staff as a whole.

The elected governor may therefor be torn between her/his own view, that of colleagues in different and shifting camps, and that of the headteacher (which may itself be neither constant nor wholly disclosed). The governor's own assessment of the issues may also, of course, adjust as the arguments are presented.

ATL suggests that the following principles should be adopted in such circumstances.

Firstly, the elected governor should fully register all the views voiced by her/his constituents, and seek to present faithfully the arguments and evidence as s/he understands them. S/he should also make known her/his personal assessment, and make it clear that this is what it is. In any vote, s/he should be sure that the other governors understand whether her/his vote is being cast to register the majority teaching staff or parent view, or to record a personal judgement, or both. Ultimately, however, her/his decision on

which way to vote must be a carefully-considered individual judgement. Finally, over matters which may be highly-controversial, elected governors should consider confining the expression of their personal views to the governing body forum. They should also give thought to the wisdom of distancing themselves from public campaigns on the matter in hand.

Whatever ATL may say on this difficult topic, one thing is obvious: the most important personal quality any elected governor needs is unquestionable integrity.

UNION REPRESENTATIVES AS ELECTED GOVERNORS

Since union representatives (usually, though not invariably, elected) already represent the individual and collective views of their members, it is not surprising that they may often be seen as obvious candidates to serve as teacher or staff governors in their school.

In their union role, these members of staff should be knowledgeable about national and local issues likely to affect the school. They will also have experience of expressing the views of colleagues and, when appropriate, negotiating on their behalf. The fact that they are union representatives implies that they carry their colleagues' confidence.

It is clearly undesirable for employee governor elections to be run along strict trade union lines, as the representative(s) with the largest membership would have an automatic 'block vote' advantage. If that became common, there would be the real risk that union representatives/teacher governors would be tempted to voice the possibly sectional interests of a particular union rather than the views of **all** members of staff, including the genuine disagreements they may have on major issues.

Teacher and staff governors (whether union representatives or not) must faithfully register the view of all their colleagues – including those who may be in a minority. Similarly, their constituents must have confidence that they will do so.

Teacher or staff governors who are also union representatives should be open about this with the governing body – and must remember that they are **elected governors first.** They should also bear in mind that, if they invariably bring to governing body discussions a predictable and pre-determined party line, their colleague governors may be tempted to discount their contributions rather than take them fully into account.

Serving as a teacher governor and acting as a union representative both often involve forming and articulating views on the same issues – but the two activities are not identical. **ATL believes that teacher governors should be elected, irrespective of their trade union affiliation, on the basis of their personal integrity and impartiality, their professional knowledge and experience, and because they are the people most likely to represent staff views as a whole.** Teacher union representatives often possess precisely these qualities, but it is unlikely that they will have a monopoly on them.

EMPLOYEE GOVERNORS: RECONCILING DIFFERENCES

The role of the headteacher and the employee governors is to represent to other governors their professional view of how the governing body's decisions will affect the school. It is important that, whenever possible, that view should be presented coherently and with firm supporting evidence.

For that reason, it is good practice for the headteacher and the teacher and staff governors to **meet informally** before governing body meetings to discuss the issues likely to arise. It is only professional courtesy for the head to inform her/his colleagues of any matter s/he proposes to raise, if this is not clear from the agenda circulated in advance. Similarly, the employee governors owe it to their headteacher to give prior notice of any issue they wish to raise for governing body decision.

Where teacher or staff governors judge that the school employees' opinion on an issue differs from that of the head, they should normally discuss the matter thoroughly with her/him **before** the governing body formally considers it. In most cases, they will be able to reconcile their difference of professional opinion, but that will not always happen.

The headteacher, although an employee, is essentially the 'manager' of the school (and the staff). Teacher and staff governors are elected to represent the views of key sections of the school staff. When the headteacher makes one assessment of an issue, and the employee governors know that the staff adopt another stance, the different viewpoints should be fully explained to the governors as a whole. The governing body can then fully debate the issue in the light of all the available professional information, and reach a decision.

Headteachers who seek to prevent the airing of genuine differences of professional judgement – and regrettably such heads do exist – are behaving improperly. It is also only fair to add that teacher or staff governors who seek to use the governing body as a forum in which to pursue anti-head campaigns act just as unprofessionally. Neither serve the interests of the school nor the employees in it.

As a school's most senior manager, a headteacher is entitled – and indeed under a duty – to inform the governing body of her/his professional judgement and the reasons for it. Employee governors have a similar responsibility to inform governors of their judgement, the evidence for it, and the extent to which it is based upon a general staff view.

Only unconfident headteachers will see that as a challenge to their managerial authority, but it is sometimes the unconfident who need to be resisted most steadfastly: there will be occasions when teacher and staff governors have to oppose, very firmly, attempts to deny them the opportunity to express their view, and thereby to obstruct the governing body's opportunity to hear their opinion.

7   THE REMOVAL OF GOVERNORS

School governors are intended to play a robust and independent role as **representatives** of their nominating or electing body, rather than as **delegates** mandated to act. This means that they are, to a large extent, protected from easy removal from office.

STATUTORY DISQUALIFICATION

There are specified circumstances in which governors are legally **disqualified** from continuing to hold office. They include bankruptcy, conviction of certain criminal offences and persistent absence. These are discussed in Chapter 4.

ELECTED GOVERNORS

For **teacher and staff governors** and **parent governors,** the position is clear: there is **no provision** in legislation for them, as elected governors, **to be removed** during their term of office. (In this respect, even parent and partnership governors who have been appointed rather than elected are regarded as having been elected.) Rather like Members of Parliament, these governors are independent once elected for their four-year term. They can be voted out at the next election, but they cannot be 'dismissed' by their constituents in the meantime. A vote of no confidence in a representative governor may put pressure on her/him to resign, but it does not have the effect of automatic removal. In short, **parent, teacher and staff governors cannot be sacked** (Regulation 18(2)).

It should be noted that if a **teacher or staff** governor ceases to be employed at the school, s/he must give up office immediately (see Appendix B, Schedule 5). However, a **parent** governor is not disqualified from continuing to serve if her/his child leaves the school during her/his term of office.

APPOINTED GOVERNORS

The issue of removal becomes more complex in the case of **appointed governors** (those nominated by LEAs or chosen – normally by a church – as foundation governors in voluntary schools). Regulation 18 of the 1999 Regulations specifies that these governors **'may be removed from office by the person or persons who appointed them'.** This may appear to give the nominating bodies totally unfettered power to dismiss their governors. In practice, the position is by no means that simple.

For example, a Dr Kuba Assegai had been appointed as a community governor by the London Borough of Brent. He was (in the judge's words) a 'large, colourful and exuberant personality'. After several disturbing incidents in 1987 – culminating in Dr Assegai physically threatening the chair of the Education Committee – the council resolved to remove him forthwith. He appealed to the High Court. The judge (in **R -v- Brent LBC ex parte Assegai 1987**) quashed his dismissal, not on the basis that it was unreasonable, but because he had been given no notice of the intended resolution, nor any opportunity to state his case on the matter.

Even in removing turbulent governors, therefor, appointing bodies must observe the rules of **natural justice.**

Two other celebrated cases demonstrate that an appointing body's apparent power of removal **cannot be used to force its governors to vote in a particular way.**

In 1988, the Haberdashers Askes Hatcham School in London was contemplating a reorganisation from voluntary-controlled status to that of a city technology college. The Inner London Education Authority (ILEA), as the maintaining body, opposed this. Following their refusal to give assurances that they would vote in accordance with this policy, two of the school's authority governors were removed by the ILEA. (It may not be coincidental that these were the two nominated by the opposition Conservative Group on the ILEA.) The case (**R -v- ILEA ex parte Brunyate 1989**) went all the way to the House of Lords. Although the Act apparently entitles appointing bodies to remove their governors at will, the Lords held that the threat of removal to enforce compliance with the wishes of the appointing body was 'an usurpation of the governors' independent function'. The governors were reinstated – and Haberdashers Askes became a city technology college.

The same principle of independence was followed in the highly-publicised Cardinal Vaughan School case (**R -v- Westminster RC Diocese Trustee ex parte Andrews**) in 1989. Here, the Roman Catholic diocese proposed to reorganise its voluntary-aided schools, removing their sixth forms and establishing a sixth form college. The Cardinal Vaughan governors objected. When two foundation governors refused to support the plan, they were removed by the diocesan trustee and replaced with more compliant appointees. The school parents' association pursued the issue, and the Court of Appeal ruled that the trustee's action **in removing foundation governors because of their**

voting intentions was unlawful. The parents subsequently voted for the school to become grant-maintained.

However, governors **appointed by the LEA** have been less successful in opposing purely **'political'** removals. When control of Warwickshire County Council changed hands after the May 1989 local elections, the incoming Conservative group resolved to remove Mrs Dill-Russell (a Liberal Democrat nominee) from her governorship of Marie Corelli Special School and to replace her with their own candidate. Not surprisingly, she resisted. However, the Court of Appeal (in **R -v- Warwickshire CC ex parte Dill-Russell 1990**) upheld the Council's action. While recognising that Mrs Dill-Russell had been unceremoniously hounded out of office through no fault of her own, the judges concluded that the party in power was entitled to introduce its own political nominees. Mrs Dill-Russell was an unfortunate 'casualty of an agreed scheme of political weighting'.

All of these cases are highlighted in Chapter 15.

The present position, then, is that most governors' tenure of office is remarkably secure. **Elected governors** cannot be removed by their 'constituents'; **appointed and foundation governors** cannot be replaced to enforce their appointing body's policy; but **LEA governors** can be removed to ensure political balance. The Code of Practice on LEA-School Relations now requires LEAs to publish the criteria and process used to identify LEA governor nominees.

However, the 'security of tenure' for **co-opted governors** has recently altered.

CO-OPTED GOVERNORS

The 1999 Regulations introduce, from September 1999, a new procedure enabling the governing body to remove **co-opted governors** (Regulations 18 and 19 – see Appendix B). Any resolution to remove a co-opted governor must comply with five requirements:

- it must be considered at **two separate governing body meetings,** held not less than 14 days apart;
- the proposal must be **specified as an item of business** on the agenda for both meetings;
- the notices of the meetings and their agendas must be sent to governors with the **full seven days' notice** (Regulation 34(6));
- each meeting must have a **quorum of at least two-thirds** of those eligible to vote (Regulation 37);
- at the second meeting, the proposer(s) must state their **reasons** and the governor in question must be given an opportunity to make a **statement in response.**

In the case of an **additional co-opted governor** (see page 8), the proposal for removal must originate from the nominating body – which must, similarly, give (written) reasons to the governing body and to the governor in question. The above procedure must then be followed. The nominating body may also make representations to the meeting (Regulation 19).

The DfEE's Guidance on the 1999 Regulations advises that the power to remove co-optees should only be used in 'exceptional circumstances, for example where there has been an irretrievable breakdown in relationships.'

FURTHER PROPOSALS ON REMOVAL

The House of Commons Education and Employment Committee's Inquiry: **The Role of School Governors** recommended in July 1999 that the DfEE should bring forward proposals enabling governing bodies to **remove 'rogue' governors** (of any category).

Its conclusions on this issue were as follows:

'50   The headteacher associations will, of course, see the worst examples of 'rogue' governors. But we do not accept that there is evidence of a widespread problem. Even if the headteacher associations are seeing a few hundred cases each year, this is still a very small proportion of the total number of school governors. Therefor, we believe that cases of 'rogue' governors are relatively infrequent. However, we recognise the significant detrimental effect that 'rogue' governors can have on a governing body and its school. The key characteristic of the 'rogue' governor is that he or she acts in a manner that disregards the corporate nature and responsibilities of the governing body. We therefor consider that, in extreme cases where the relationship between an individual governor and the majority of the governing body has irretrievably broken down, there should be mechanisms to remove governors from the governing body, and that these should apply to all categories of governor. We stress that such

mechanisms should be used only in cases of last resort. We acknowledge the risk highlighted by Mrs Sallis that in some cases the apparently 'rogue' governor is, in fact, pursuing a perfectly proper line of argument. We would not wish to see governors removed simply because they do not fall into line with the majority view of the governing body. Therefor, we recommend that proceedings to remove individual governors, apart from reasons of non-attendance, should be restricted to clearly defined cases. Later in our report we recommend that governing bodies adopt a code of practice covering the relations between the head and governors, governors' conduct in the school, etc (see paragraphs 61-64). Only in cases where there has been a clear breach of this code of practice would we recommend that procedures to remove a governor be invoked. We recommend that the DfEE bring forward proposals to allow all categories of governor to be removed from office. We would expect that such an action would require at least two-thirds of those eligible to vote to support a resolution removing the governor from office. Any mechanism would have to take account of the principles of natural justice.'

(The Inquiry's summary of its recommendations is set out in Appendix C.)

ATL has strong reservations about this proposal, particularly in the case of elected governors, where the capacity to remove them would, we consider, run counter to the principle of democracy.

REMOVAL OF THE CHAIR

Governing bodies have the power to remove the chair of governors from office without waiting for the annual election at the first governors' meeting of the school year. This is set out in Regulation 30 of the 1999 Regulations (see Appendix B). However, again five restrictions normally apply here:

■ a resolution to remove the chair must be confirmed at a **second governors' meeting** held at least 14 days after the first one;

■ the question of the chair's removal must be a **specified item of business** on the agendas of both meetings;

■ the notices of the meetings and their agendas must be sent to governors with the full **seven days' notice** (Regulation 34(6));

■ the **quorum** for each meeting must be two-thirds of those eligible to vote (Regulation 37);

■ at the second meeting, the proposer(s) must give **reasons** for their recommendation that the chair be removed and s/he must be given an opportunity to make **a statement in response**.

Where additional governors have been appointed under the LEA's or the Secretary of State's powers of intervention (see Chapter 13), only two formalities apply: the chair's removal must be specified as an item of business on the agenda for the meeting, and the quorum for the removal decision is one-half of the governors entitled to vote (Regulations 30(4) and 37).

There is no comparable procedure for the removal of the **vice-chair**.

Removal from the position of chair under these procedures does **not** imply removal as a governor.

THE CLERK TO THE GOVERNORS

The 1999 Regulations include significant new provisions concerning the clerk to the governing body. In community and voluntary-controlled (VC) schools, the LEA must appoint as clerk the person selected by the governing body; in foundation and voluntary schools, the governors appoint the clerk direct (Regulation 23 – see Appendix B). In either case, from 1 April 2000, neither the headteacher nor any other governor can be clerk – save for a particular meeting in the clerk's absence (Regulation 22).

There are also new measures as to the **dismissal of the clerk** (Regulation 24). In contrast to the procedure for the removal of governors, there is no 'natural justice' requirement in the Regulations for reasons to be given to the individual, nor do the Regulations give her/him a specific opportunity to respond. However, Regulation 21 provides that these provisions as to the dismissal of the clerk are 'without prejudice to any rights and liabilities which the clerk may have if s/he is employed under a contract of employment'. In community and VC schools, the LEA must dismiss the clerk on receipt of written notification (with reasons) from the governing body. In foundation and VA schools, the governors merely 'determine that the clerk should be dismissed'.

In community and VC schools where the school's delegated budget has been withdrawn (see Chapter 13), the LEA appoints and dismisses the clerk following such consultations with the governors as it thinks fit. In the case of foundation and VA schools operating without a delegated budget, the governors can only appoint or dismiss the clerk with the LEA's consent and the LEA can direct her/his dismissal (Regulation 25).

Governing body decisions as to the appointment or dismissal of the clerk may be delegated to a committee but not to an individual (Regulation 42(5)).

8 GOVERNORS' RIGHTS AND LIABILITIES

THE GOVERNORS' CONSTITUTIONAL POSITION

Governing bodies are vested with a bewildering range of both **powers** (from hiring and firing of staff to the control of public money running into millions of pounds) and **responsibilities** (extending from statutory obligations as to the curriculum to setting standards of behaviour for pupils). The system of school governance represents a truly remarkable exercise (and act of public faith) in lay trusteeship. Governors are, in essence, **committed amateurs**.

The division of powers between LEA, governing body and headteacher is ill-defined. The traditional position (confirmed in Section 130 of the 1996 Act) is that the governing body controls the general conduct of the school, but that the headteacher controls its day-to-day management and organisation – including the deployment and direction of staff. Put simply, the governors decide the school's **policy**, while the head is responsible for **operational** matters. These are separate but complementary tasks. It is crucially important that everyone involved recognises this as a **partnership** which needs to work well in practice for the good of the

school. However, the inter-relationship is sometimes uneasy. The Government is planning to publish Terms of Reference Regulations in the near future, which will hopefully clarify these issues further.

In the meantime, one thing is clear: powers and responsibilities are placed upon the governors collectively as a corporate body. Only where decisions or powers have been explicitly delegated to an individual governor (or to a committee) do they have specific authority to act on behalf of the governing body as a whole. In short, the **governing body has power, but governors as individuals do not**. Governors need to be careful not to misunderstand their role.

Governors visiting classrooms

A recurring example is the question of **governors visiting classrooms**. It is clearly valuable for governors to acquaint themselves with the school, and to gain a first-hand impression of its premises, its work, its staff and its teaching – and this can best be achieved by planned and organised visits arranged with the headteacher. However, individual governors have no entitlement to 'inspect' teaching. To arrive at a classroom with this intention would be at best insensitive and at worst intrusive and counter-productive. Governors who visit classrooms should recognise that they do so as **observers, not inspectors**.

Governors' codes of practice

In considering their constitutional position, individuals (and, perhaps, elected governors in particular) should keep in mind that, having accepted the role of governor, they must accept **collective responsibility** for decisions made. They cannot act effectively as a member of the metaphorical 'team' but at the same time stand on the touchline and heckle.

The Report of the Parliamentary Education and Employment Committee's **Inquiry** into **The Role of School Governors** (July 1999) recommends that governing bodies should adopt a **code of practice for governors** which outlines the appropriate relationship between individual governors, the whole governing body and the school. The code would also cover the appropriate conduct of governors in the school. The report proposes that the DfEE should develop a model code of practice in consultation with all involved organisations. ATL welcomes this initiative. The report's summary of recommendations is reproduced as Appendix C.

Turning to the governing body's relations with the **local authority**, the DfEE (utilising powers under Section 127 of the SSFA 1998) has published a statutory **Code of Practice on LEA-School Relations**. This includes helpful guidance, emphasising the importance of 'developing through partnership a culture in which schools will want to work with the LEA'. The advice is particularly valuable as to situations where difficulties arise and the authority contemplates using its powers of intervention (see Chapter 13).

ALLOWANCES

From September 1999, new Regulations enable maintained school governing bodies to establish a scheme for the payment of **expense allowances** to governors, and to non-governor members of committees. The expenses which may be reimbursed are those 'necessarily incurred' for the purposes of enabling the individual to perform any duty. This extends the previous capacity to repay only travel and subsistence expenditure now to include such items as childcare costs and other out-of-pocket expenses. However, there is **no capacity to pay an attendance allowance**. Governors are not entitled to be paid for their services.

The governors' allowance scheme should set the rate(s) for payment but, in the case of travel and subsistence, this cannot exceed the rate set by the Secretary of State for local government purposes. Further, the scheme cannot set different rates for different governors or other recipients. The Report of the Parliamentary Inquiry urges individual governing bodies to implement an expense allowance scheme (see Appendix C).

In the case of schools without delegated budgets, the LEA is empowered to make a comparable scheme (The Education (Governors' Allowances) Regulations 1999, SI 1999 No 703).

TIME OFF

Governors of maintained schools have a statutory right to take **'reasonable time off'** from work to carry out their public duties. The relevant legislation does not specify what is 'reasonable', but states that the requirements of the public duty, the circumstances of the employer's business and the effect on it of the employee's absence (and any time off already granted for other public or union duties) are all relevant factors. There is, in fact, no legal obligation on the employer to give **paid** time off for this absence, although most public (and many private) employers do grant time off with pay.

The duties for which governors are entitled to take time off are defined by the Act as attendance at meetings of the governing body or its committee, and 'any other thing approved' by the governing body. This is likely to include approved school visits and training for governors.

If a governor is refused reasonable time off, her/his remedy is to bring a claim in the employment tribunal within three months.

TRAINING FOR GOVERNORS

Governors are legally entitled to receive from their local authority, free of charge, both:

■ **information** – including a copy of the school's Instrument of Government; and

■ such **training** as the LEA 'considers appropriate'

(Regulation 5 of the 1999 Regulations and Schedule 11, SSFA 1998). Grants are available to LEAs for this purpose and many (but unfortunately by no means all) local authorities provide highly-effective governor training and support programmes.

Training is not presently compulsory – although the Parliamentary Inquiry recommends that **induction training** should be made compulsory for new governors and newly-appointed chairs of governing bodies (again, see Appendix C). ATL supports these proposals.

PERSONAL LIABILITY

The financial and legal responsibilities of governing bodies are significant, and understandable concerns exist about the extent to which individual governors could be held personally liable for their decisions. In fact, the legislation affords school governors considerable protection. Firstly, schools now have formal **corporate status:** they are legal entities in their own right. This means that claims against the governors will almost invariably be pursued against the governing body as a corporate body rather than against the chair or other individual governors in a personal capacity or as 'trustees'. Secondly, Section 50(7) of the SSFA 1998 provides that governors of maintained schools with a delegated budget 'shall **not incur any personal liability** in respect of anything done **in good faith** in the exercise, or purported exercise' of their power to spend the budget delegated to them 'as they think fit for the purposes of the school'.

The risk of governors facing claims as individuals is very small. Nevertheless, ATL's advice is that they should **arrange insurance cover** for this (remote) risk of personal liability.

Employers of staff and managers of premises are obliged to maintain insurance to cover their potential liability for loss or injury to third parties (including pupils and visitors). In most maintained schools this will normally be arranged through the local authority. However, **ATL urges governors to ensure that their governing body** (whether through the LEA or otherwise, as appropriate) **has arranged appropriate insurance** to provide cover not only for the more obvious risks, such as negligence and public/employer's liability, but also for other potential claims such as those for defamation of character.

This insurance should cover not only the governing body's 'corporate' liability, but also the (remote) risk of a claim being pursued against an individual governor in a personal capacity.

CRIMINAL LIABILITY

Governors should be aware that, in certain circumstances, the governing body can incur criminal liability. Its obligations under health and safety legislation and for the care of school vehicles, for instance, must be taken very seriously.

For example, in May 1994, the governors of a grant-maintained school were fined more than £2,000 by magistrates after a school minibus crashed on a science trip. The vehicle had been used without proper insurance, with no public service vehicle permit, and with flat tyres. The teacher driving was also fined and disqualified from driving for 12 months. Needless to say, it is not possible to obtain insurance against potential criminal liability.

Since the publication of Lord Nolan's Report **Standards in Public Life** in 1997, there has been renewed emphasis on public servants undertaking their duties with honesty, integrity and openness. The report sets out seven principles:

Selflessness
Holders of public office should take decisions solely in terms of the public interest. They should not do so in order to gain financial or other material benefits for themselves, their family, or their friends.

Integrity
Holders of public office should not place themselves under any financial or other obligation to outside individuals or organisations that might influence them in the performance of their official duties.

Objectivity
In carrying out public business, including making public appointments, awarding contracts, or recommending individuals for rewards and benefits, holders of public office should make choices on merit.

Accountability
Holders of public office are accountable for their decisions and actions to the public and must submit themselves to whatever scrutiny is appropriate to their office.

Openness
Holders of public office should be as open as possible about all the decisions and actions that they take. They should give reasons for their decisions and restrict information only when the wider public interest clearly demands it.

Honesty

Holders of public office have a duty to declare any private interests relating to their public duties and to take steps to resolve any conflicts arising in a way that protects the public interest.

Leadership

Holders of public office should promote and support these principles by leadership and example.

These have become known as the 'Nolan principles'. The report essentially addressed the activities of national and local government. However, it is becoming widely accepted that these principles should be observed generally by those responsible for spending public money – including school governors. ATL supports this approach.

REGISTER OF INTERESTS

One element of the need to observe these principles of selflessness, integrity and openness is the advisability of schools maintaining a **register of pecuniary interests.** In January 1999, the DfEE issued statutory guidance to local authorities as to the content of local management schemes for schools. This includes a requirement that governing bodies must, by 31 December 1999, establish a Register listing the business interests of each governor and the headteacher.

This Register of Interests should record pecuniary interests (such as directorships, significant shareholdings and involvement as a partner or an employee) including those held by their spouse/partner or members of their immediate family. It should be open to inspection by governors, staff, parents and the LEA – and should be updated annually.

There has been some debate as to whether the Register should include the interests of **all** staff in the school. ATL's view is that a sensible balance should be struck between observing the Nolan principles – ensuring integrity in the spending of public money – and avoiding unwarranted intrusion into an individual's essentially private affairs. Accordingly, ATL does not consider it necessary or appropriate for staff who do not make material management or financial decisions (eg appointing staff or spending a budget) to be included in a Register of Interests.

9 PROCEEDINGS OF GOVERNING BODIES

From September 1999, the rules as to the governance of schools have been extended to provide a largely common system for all maintained schools. For ease of reference, the new School Government Regulations (referred to throughout this guide as 'the 1999 Regulations') are set out in Appendix B.

Schools no longer have Articles of Government, since the provisions they formerly contained have been subsumed either in various recent Education Acts, such as the 1996 Education Act (the 1996 Act), the 1998 School Standards and Framework Act (the SSFA), or in the 1999 Regulations. Governing bodies are empowered to regulate their own procedure and that of their committees (Schedule 11 of the SSFA 1998). Some – such as former grant-maintained schools – have established **standing orders** clarifying their own rules, but there is now no legal obligation for schools to do so.

However, in all their proceedings – convening and running meetings, establishing committees, delegating power and making decisions – **governing bodies must now observe the 1999 Regulations**. The main requirements are as follows:

THE POSITION OF CHAIR

The governing body **must elect a chair and vice-chair** at its first meeting of the school year (Regulation 29). Teacher and staff governors (and any other governors employed at the school, such as the headteacher) are not eligible for these roles. In a similar way, they are precluded from acting as chair or vice-chair of a governing body committee. If both the chair and vice-chair are absent, the governing body elects a chair for that particular meeting.

The 1999 Regulations introduce some further formalities into the process for **electing the chair** (and vice-chair) from 1 April 2000 – perhaps because, in some governing bodies, this has previously been done casually or 'on the nod'. Under this new procedure, the clerk must **invite nominations** prior to the meeting and **list the candidates** for the position in the agenda sent out before the meeting.

Governors may nominate themselves. If no nominations are listed on the agenda, nominations will be taken at the meeting. The clerk must act as chairman during the election of the chair (but does not have a casting vote). Significantly, any contested election for the position of chair or vice-chair must be decided by secret ballot – with the nominees withdrawing and not voting (Regulation 29).

The chair of governors has an important position. First and foremost, s/he presides over governing body meetings. S/he should enjoy the full confidence of her/his colleague governors. As the National Association of Governors and Managers puts it: 'An effective governing body operates with the minimum of formality, under the guidance of the chair who moves business on, allows every governor a reasonable say but discourages unnecessary repetition of what a paper contains, or somebody else has already said, and secures a clear outcome, which is recorded in promptly circulated minutes and is conscientiously implemented'.

The chair is given certain specific responsibilities in **particular circumstances** (eg concerning pupil exclusions, complaints procedures, teacher appraisal and LEA reports of concern about the headteacher).

However, chairs must not act as if they have autocratic powers, over and beyond their position as a governor. They should see themselves essentially as *primus inter pares* (first among equals). The chair, for example, is not in normal circumstances entitled to make decisions 'on behalf of the governors'. In fact, the chair of governors (or the vice-chair in her/his absence) is given only three general powers in the Regulations:

- the right to a second or **casting vote** where there is an equal division of votes (Regulation 38);
- the capacity to **act in cases of urgency** on behalf of the governing body, ie where delay would be 'likely to be seriously detrimental' to the interests of the school, or to a parent, pupil or employee (Regulation 43). 'Delay' here means delay beyond when it would be reasonably practicable to convene a meeting of the governing body or its committee as appropriate. However, the chair cannot take action in this way on matters which the governing body cannot delegate (see Chapter 10). Furthermore, any 'chair's action' taken under this 'emergency' power must be reported to the next governing body meeting; and
- the authority to give directions to the clerk as to the **convening of meetings** – including calling them at short notice (Regulation 34).

Clearly, the chair of governors has influence, can take initiatives (such as bringing matters before the governing body), and often acts as the governors' spokesperson. Nevertheless, **while acting as the governing body's 'leader', the chair must not attempt to act as its 'president'.**

There is a procedure for the **removal of the chair** from office (Regulation 30). This is discussed in Chapter 7.

CONVENING MEETINGS – AGENDAS AND NOTICE

Governing bodies must meet **at least once a term** (Regulation 34), but **any three**

governors can requisition a special meeting by notifying the clerk in writing.

Meetings are to be convened by the clerk, giving **seven clear days' written notice** to governors both of the meeting and its **agenda** – unless the chair (or in her/his absence, the vice-chair) decides that shorter notice may be given because 'there are matters demanding urgent consideration' (Regulation 34(5). However, the chair's discretion to shorten the notice of meetings does not apply where a proposal for the removal of the chair, or the removal of a co-opted governor, is to be considered (Regulation 34(6)).

A copy of the notice of the meeting and its agenda must be sent to the LEA and (if s/he is not a governor) the headteacher.

A meeting is not invalidated if an individual governor has not received written notice or a copy of the agenda.

Under Section 162 and Schedule 18 of the Education Act 1996, the governing body is obliged (save at some hospitals and boarding schools) to hold an **annual parents' meeting** to which all parents are invited. The purpose is to discuss the **governors' annual report** to parents, as well as action taken by the governing body, the head and the LEA to fulfil their duties. The meeting can pass resolutions which the governing body must consider, provided that the number of parents present is equal to at least 20 per cent of the number of registered pupils.

ADJOURNMENTS

Regulation 36 makes clear that a meeting must be terminated if it is – or becomes – **inquorate** (see below). If the number of governors present falls below the quorum before the agenda has been completed, a further meeting must be convened 'as soon as is reasonably practicable'. The governing body also has **power to adjourn** a meeting before completing its business, but in this case it must set a time and date for the reconvened meeting before doing so – which need not comply with the normal requirement for the seven days' notice of meetings (Regulation 36(5)).

QUORUM

In accordance with Regulation 37, the normal quorum for governing body meetings is **one-third** (rounded up to a whole number of the total membership of the governing body when complete – ie vacancies are counted in the total), subject to a **minimum of three governors**. However, a higher quorum of **two-thirds** is required for several specific purposes:

■ **co-opting** governors;

■ **appointing** parent or partnership **governors**;

■ **appointing members to a committee;**

■ determining any question relating to a committee (eg **delegating** powers to it) – see Chapter 10;

■ voting to **remove a co-opted** (or additional co-opted) **governor**;

■ voting to **remove the chair;**

■ arranging for an Education Action Forum to discharge any function of the governing body.

Note that the calculation for this higher quorum is slightly different: it is two-thirds of the number of governors who are **entitled to vote**. Any vacancies are therefor ignored here. Furthermore, this means that, when voting for co-opted places, any

existing co-opted governors (who do not have a vote on this issue) are also disregarded in setting the quorum.

TAKING DECISIONS

Decisions are taken by a majority of votes of those attending and voting on a proposal. In the case of a tie, the chair (or acting chair) has a second or casting vote (Regulation 38).

RESCINDING RESOLUTIONS

Governing bodies are able to **vary** or **rescind** resolutions, but the proposal to do so must be notified as a **specific item of business** on the agenda for the meeting at which the variation or rescission is to be considered (Regulation 35 of the 1999 Regulations). Note that the Regulations do not require a higher than normal quorum for this.

PUBLIC ACCESS TO MEETINGS

Governing body meetings are not automatically open to the public (or the press). Regulation 33 makes clear that the governors are **entitled to decide** whether anyone who is not a governor (other than the clerk or the headteacher) should be allowed to attend. Where the head has chosen not to be a governor, s/he has an automatic right (under Regulation 32) to attend governing body meetings, subject to any conflict of interest arising (see Chapter 14).

PUBLICATION OF AGENDAS, MINUTES ETC

Governing bodies are required by the School Government Regulations ('the

1999 Regulations') to keep formal written minutes, including a full record of attendance showing both governors and observers (see Regulation 39). The minutes must be approved by the governors either at the meeting in question, or the next meeting, and signed by the chair. They must be kept in a book (which may be loose-leaf, provided each page is numbered and signed).

Significantly, these minutes are open to the public. The draft **minutes** (once approved by the chair), together with the **agenda** and any report, document or other paper considered at a governing body meeting, **must be made available at the school 'to persons wishing to inspect them'** as soon as is reasonably practicable (see Regulation 40). The same general rule applies to the minutes and papers for governors' committees (Regulation 55). However, the governors are entitled to decide to deal with certain issues **in confidence** (see below), in which case the relevant section of the 'public' minutes should contain only those aspects of the discussion or decision which they agree should be widely known.

None of the legislative rules specifies a timescale within which the approved minutes of any meeting should be prepared. In practice, because of intervals between meetings, there is sometimes considerable delay, even though the Regulations provide for draft minutes to be made available once they have been approved by the chair. **Wherever possible, however, delay should be avoided.**

What should be resisted is any attempt to prevent elected governors reporting (orally or in writing) to their colleagues, not because the issues are confidential, **but simply because the minutes have yet to be confirmed.**

When governors are discouraged from reporting matters which are not, nor should be, confidential, the effect is to deny those who elected them early access to information and the opportunity for legitimate discussion. If elected governors are unable to report back to their 'constituency' until the minutes have been formally confirmed, the points at issue will frequently have become academic because they have been overtaken by events and the mere passage of time. Where attempts to delay the dissemination of information and thus to stifle discussion are deliberate – and sometimes they are – this constitutes a clear abuse.

The underlying philosophy of the legislation has been to increase and widen the participation of all the groups represented on governing bodies, including parents and employees, so that properly-balanced decisions emerge and the flow of information is enhanced.

ATL considers that governors are free to report back to their 'constituents' accurately and promptly on all issues which are not specifically designated confidential. However, when doing so, they should respect the principle of governors' 'collective responsibility' for governing body decisions (see page 27).

CONFIDENTIAL ISSUES

There are, of course, certain issues over which the deliberations and votes of a governing body (or one of its committees) should be conducted in confidence. However, it must be emphasised that these circumstances are very much the exception rather than the rule. It would be an abuse for a governing body to propose a blanket imposition of confidentiality on all its meetings and proceedings.

The provisions governing confidentiality (Regulation 40(2)) state that the governing body (or its committee) may exclude from the normal requirement for publication any material relating to:

■ a named teacher or other person employed, or proposed to be employed, at the school;

■ a named pupil at, or a candidate for admission to, the school; and

■ any matter which, by reason of its nature, the governing body is satisfied should remain confidential.

This latter point makes it clear that no issues are automatically confidential. A specific **decision** should be made by the governing body (or committee) in each case – following a discussion and a vote, as appropriate.

The Regulations clearly intend that **disciplinary cases** concerning employees or pupils, **complaints**, questions concerning the **appointment or dismissal** of staff, and **admissions** or **exclusions** of pupils should all be dealt with on a confidential basis and in camera. ('In camera' means that only members of the governing body are present at the discussion, ie that other persons – including members of the press – are excluded.) Only the operative decision, once reached, should be reported in the governors' publicly-available minutes. ATL argues that the process of **teacher appraisal** (and the documents associated with it) should also be dealt with confidentially. DFE Circular 12/91 advises that appraisal records should be confidential, with only the chair of governors having access to the summary.

Other cases are either difficult to categorise, or are more open to genuine differences of view and judgement.

Whatever the issues may be, however, ATL believes strongly that **it should be normal practice for the chair of a governing body, after consultation with the clerk, to notify members in advance of those matters s/he proposes to deal with on a confidential basis (and/or in camera).** In most cases, it will be possible to give this prior indication when notice of a meeting and the agenda are provided with seven clear days' notice, as required by legislation. On some occasions, however, it may not be possible to raise the issue of confidentiality until the meeting itself.

Wherever possible and appropriate, the chair should give the reasons for her/his proposal, and **allow debate and a vote** on the matter if the proposed ruling is controversial. Wherever another governor proposes that a particular item should be dealt with on a confidential basis, or that a matter be taken in camera, the chair should similarly allow an opportunity for discussion and a vote on the suggestion.

In real life, it must be acknowledged that a discussion which does not seem likely to involve confidential issues can sometimes come to do so as it develops. Here, it is most important for the chair to indicate as soon as possible whether s/he judges that some, or all, of the discussion should be treated as confidential to the governors (and, if necessary, allow debate and a vote on that proposal).

No discussion of an individual employee's conduct or competence should take place outside the cloak of confidentiality, or without sufficient advance notification to the member of staff concerned. Indeed, it is in any event most unwise for **specific complaints about an employee** (or a pupil) to be discussed in a full governing body meeting, since this could prejudice the individual governors who may in due course have to consider the issue formally at a hearing. The chair should curtail discussion of such issues.

Once the governing body has decided to treat a matter as confidential, this decision should be interpreted as binding on **all** governors, including elected governors. Staff and parents should not invite, far less press, elected governors to breach that confidentiality.

Nevertheless, there is no such thing as half-open government. There should always be a substantial, identifiable reason for the governors' proceedings to be confidential and/or in camera. The fact that the subject they are considering is likely to cause controversy or public disagreement (eg the school's possible re-organisation or change of status) is not, of itself, sufficient justification for the imposition of confidentiality.

10 GOVERNORS' COMMITTEES AND RULES ON DELEGATION

DELEGATION OF POWERS

Governing bodies have – and normally use – discretion to **delegate** many significant management powers to a committee, an individual governor, or the headteacher.

However, Regulation 42 of the 1999 Regulations establishes several controls on this general power to delegate. There are some powers which may **not** be delegated – and others which the governing body **must** delegate.

Restrictions on delegation

The main functions which **must not be delegated** and which must be dealt with by the **full governing body** are as follows:

- **appointing** parent or co-opted governors or **removing** co-opted governors;
- approving the annual **budget plan**;
- approving the **annual report to parents**;
- approving the school **prospectus**;

- **appointing the chair** and vice-chair;
- **removing the chair**;
- decisions on **delegating functions** and establishing **committees** and selection panels;
- decisions on **school session times** (and – in foundation and VA schools – dates of terms and holidays);
- appointing a selection panel for the **appointment of a headteacher** or deputy headteacher – and considering the panel's recommendations;
- decisions on **regulating** the governing body's (or its committees') **procedure**;
- making arrangements for **appeals** against dismissals;
- decisions on **sex education**;
- decisions on **collective worship**;
- ensuring the prohibition of **political indoctrination** and the balanced treatment of political issues;
- decisions on **home-school agreements**;
- decisions on **school discipline** policies;

- considering an **alteration**, discontinuance or change of category of the school;
- considering and setting **admission arrangements and numbers**;
- considering the preparation or variation of the school's **Instrument of Government**;
- considering the delegation of functions to an Education Action Forum.

'Compulsory' delegation to committees

There are three functions which the governing body is **required to delegate** to **specific committees** (which it is obliged to establish). These are:
- the **dismissal of staff**. Dismissals must be considered by a **staff dismissal committee** normally comprising at least three governors, and any appeal by a **dismissal appeal committee** of at least the same number (Regulations 42(2) and 47 – and see Chapter 12);
- the **exclusion of pupils** – and their reinstatement. These must be considered by the **pupil discipline committee** comprising either three or five governors (and not including the headteacher nor any non-governors), with a quorum of three. The committee's chair can take decisions on its behalf if the excluded pupil would otherwise lose an opportunity to take a public examination (Regulations 42(3) and 48);
- **consideration of complaints**. Governing bodies are required to establish complaints procedures which include a **complaints committee** to consider certain urgent or serious complaints – or appeals against decisions at earlier stages. This

committee must comprise three or more people, with a majority of governors, at least one parent and at least one non-governor. The headteacher cannot be a member (The Education (School Government) (General Complaints Procedures) Regulations 1999).

Delegation to a committee only

Further, there are some powers which the governors **may delegate to a committee, but not to an individual** (eg the chair or headteacher). These are set out in Regulation 42(5). The key ones are:
- decisions on the **admission** of particular children – which may be delegated to an **'admissions committee'** comprising the headteacher and at least two governors. Again there cannot be any non-governor members (Regulations 42(4) and 49);
- considering and setting **attendance targets**;
- appealing to the Secretary of State against a **school attendance order** concerning a particular child;
- appealing to the Secretary of State against an **LEA decision to admit a child** to the school;
- decisions on the appointment or dismissal of the **clerk**.

Decisions on any delegation of powers must be taken by the **full governing body** and are subject to a **quorum of two-thirds** (see page 34).

Regulation 41 makes clear that, where the governors have made an optional delegation of a function to a committee, this does not prevent them from exercising the same function as a full governing body.

THE OPERATION OF COMMITTEES

Subject to the rules outlined above, the governing body may establish 'such committees as it thinks fit' to fulfil its functions. The constitutions, membership and terms of reference of committees are generally a matter for the governing body to decide. They must be reviewed at least once a year. However, the 1999 Regulations establish some statutory requirements as to committees' operation:

■ the rules as to **notice** and **agendas** (Regulation 52), taking **decisions** (Regulation 53), keeping **minutes** (Regulation 54), the **publication** of papers, decisions on **confidential** items (Regulation 55), **access to the public** (Regulation 56), withdrawals (Regulation 57) and **disqualifications** from serving (Regulation 50) are all broadly the same for committees as those applicable to the full governing body (see Chapter 9 for an explanation of these rules);

■ the governing body **must appoint a clerk** to any committee established to deal with staff dismissal hearings or appeals, pupil discipline or admissions to the school. From April 2000, neither the headteacher, any other governor nor a member of the committee can act as clerk to these 'statutory' committees – save for a particular meeting in the clerk's absence (Regulation 51). For other committees, there is a **discretion** whether or not to appoint a clerk – and these restrictions on eligibility do not apply. The clerk to a committee can be dismissed by the governing body;

■ committees must have a governor as **chair**, who has a second or casting vote where necessary (Regulation 53). No teacher or staff governor (nor any other employee of the school – including the headteacher) can act as chair of a committee (Regulations 46(2)). The Regulations do not give committee chairs 'emergency' powers to act on behalf of their committees in cases of urgency (see page 33);

■ committees **can include non-governors**, provided that governors form a majority. Further, the governing body can decide that some or all of these 'external' committee members shall have **voting rights** – provided that no decision is taken by a committee unless a majority of its members present are governors (Regulation 46(2)). However, any non-governor members of staff dismissal or dismissal appeal committees are not entitled to vote (Regulation 47). Non-governor members cannot act as chairs of committees;

■ the **headteacher** (subject to any conflict of interest arising – see Chapter 14) is entitled to attend any meeting of a committee (Regulation 56).

Committees (and individuals) who have taken decisions under delegated powers must **report back** to the governing body at its next meeting (Regulation 44).

MEMBERSHIP OF COMMITTEES

It is common for governing bodies to establish committees on a wide range of their financial, curriculum and managerial functions – either to make recommendations or to take decisions under delegated powers. Indeed, much of the significant business of the governing body is organised through its committees. They are at the core of its operation. It is vitally important that all categories of governor take a full part in this.

There are certain disqualifications which apply specifically to the teacher and staff governors: ie they cannot act as chair of a committee, nor participate in decisions on staff pay or appraisal. However, subject to these – and the general requirements on withdrawing in cases of pecuniary interest, which apply to all governors (see Chapter 14) – there is no reason why employee governors should not serve on committees or working parties. **ATL believes that, wherever possible, the composition of committees should reflect the balance of interests represented on the governing body as a whole.**

For instance, there is no general legal prohibition on teacher or staff governors serving on committees dealing with appointments and dismissals of staff.

It is certainly wholly undesirable for committees to operate as inner cabinets from which the employee governors are permanently excluded.

Neither employee governors nor indeed any other category of governor should be expected to accept a rubber-stamping role within the full governing body, voting on recommendations devised within private caucus meetings. Such a practice would militate against the spirit of the Education Acts and the clear intentions of the law-makers.

11 APPOINTING STAFF

Under local management schemes, governing bodies in maintained schools control the procedures for selecting and appointing staff. Once the governors have chosen a candidate, the local authority cannot override their decision unless the proposed appointee fails to meet minimum **'staff qualification requirements'**, eg s/he does not possess qualified teacher status, does not satisfy health requirements, or has been barred from teaching.

However, the SSFA 1998 sets out (from September 1999) new rules as to the **procedure** for appointing staff and new powers for the LEA over the **appointment of headteachers**. These provisions are contained in Schedule 16 of the Act for community and voluntary-controlled (VC)

schools and Schedule 17 for foundation and voluntary-aided (VA) schools. The key provisions on appointment are as follows:

HEADTEACHER AND DEPUTY APPOINTMENTS

The governing body **must**:
- **notify the LEA** of the vacancy in writing;
- **advertise** the vacancy in national publications;
- appoint a **selection panel** of at least three governors (unless, in the case of a VA school, the governing body decides to undertake the selection itself without a panel);

- in the case of headteacher appointments, **notify the LEA** of the shortlisted candidates – and consider any representations from the authority as to their suitability;
- **interview** the candidates via this panel (save, as above, in VA schools);
- **consider the recommendations** of the panel for an appointment (save, as above, in VA schools). This function cannot be delegated to a committee;
- in community and VC schools, allow the LEA's **Chief Education Officer (CEO)** or her/his representative to **attend all proceedings** of the governing body and/or the panel as to shortlisting, interviewing and considering the appointment – and consider her/his advice.

In the case of foundation and VA schools, the governors can **decide** whether or not to accord the CEO these advisory rights (although the Secretary of State has a reserve power to impose them). Where the CEO has advisory rights in a VA school, the diocesan authority acquires similar rights;

- in the case of deputy head appointments, consider the **advice of the headteacher** (note that the present head does not have a right to advise on the appointment of her/his successor).

Where a vacancy for a headteacher is not filled by the date when the post becomes vacant, the governors **must** appoint an **acting head**, but may engage a person in this role otherwise than as an employee. In the case of a deputy, they **may** appoint an acting deputy – and on a similar basis.

In all maintained schools, the **LEA** is now entitled to **advise a headteacher selection panel** (or the governors where, in a VA school, they are acting directly) in writing that a shortlisted candidate is **not suitable**. The panel must consider any such representations and reply in writing. However, the LEA cannot refuse to appoint the governing body's chosen candidate once it has responded.

OTHER TEACHER APPOINTMENTS

When appointing to a vacancy expected to last for more than four months, the governing body:
- **must draw up a job description** in consultation with the headteacher;
- **must send a copy to the LEA;**
- **may delegate any appointment function** to one or more governors and/or to the headteacher;
- **must advertise the vacancy** *unless* **the governors**
    – **accept an LEA nominee,** or
    – **appoint an internal candidate;**
- if the post has been advertised, **must interview** such candidates as it thinks fit (the interviewees may include LEA nominees);
- **must**, in community and VC schools, allow the LEA's **Chief Education Officer** (CEO), or her/his representative, to attend all proceedings as to shortlisting, interviewing and deciding on the appointment, and must **consider her/his advice**. In the case of foundation and VA schools, the governors can **decide** whether or not to accord the CEO these advisory rights (subject to the Secretary of State's reserve power to impose them).

Where a vacancy (or a postholder's absence) is not expected to last for more than four months, the governing body may engage a person otherwise than as an employee.

Here, the Schedules to the SSFA 1998 set out very few requirements. The governing body:

- **must consult the headteacher;**
- **may advertise** (but need not);
- **may interview** (but need not);
- **may delegate any appointment function** to one or more governors and/or to the headteacher;
- **may decide the duties, hours of work** (if part-time) **and salary grade** (subject to any discretion as to grading).

12 DISCIPLINE AND DISMISSAL OF STAFF

Since the introduction of local management, governing bodies (rather than the maintaining LEA) have been responsible for the key staffing decisions in their schools: in short they have the **power to 'hire and fire'**. The SSFA 1998 now requires all maintained schools to establish both **grievance** procedures and **disciplinary rules and procedures** – which must include arrangements for dealing with 'capability' (ie competence) – and to make these procedures known to staff.

DISMISSAL

The new School Government Regulations ('the 1999 Regulations') make clear that decisions on the dismissal of staff must now be delegated to a **staff dismissal committee** and any appeal must be heard by a **dismissal appeal committee** (Regulation 47 – see Appendix B). These issues cannot be decided by the governing body as a whole, nor delegated to the headteacher or another individual. The staff dismissal committee must comprise **at least three governors**, unless there are exceptional circumstances (for example, if

there are insufficient governors to participate) – in which case it may have only two members. Furthermore, the appeal committee must contain at least the same number of governors as the committee that made the original decision.

The **headteacher** (who has a right under Schedules 16 and 17 of the SSFA 1998 to attend to give advice) cannot be a member of either of these committees. Furthermore, any non-governor member is not entitled to vote on any dismissal or appeal decision.

Where governors are considering the dismissal of a member of staff, the SSFA 1998 sets out certain **requirements which must**, at the very least, **be observed**. It is Schedule 16 of the 1998 Act which now establishes the minimum procedures for community and voluntary-controlled (VC) schools, and Schedule 17 for foundation and voluntary-aided (VA) schools. In concise form, the rules are as follows:

Community and voluntary-controlled schools

- The employee must be given a **right to a personal hearing** by the staff dismissal committee before the decision is made;
- s/he must be given an opportunity **to appeal** against the decision to the dismissal appeal committee **before** the governors notify the LEA to issue the notice of dismissal (which it must then do within 14 days);
- the **headteacher** and the **Chief Education Officer** to the LEA (or her/his representative) are **entitled to attend** any hearing or meeting to give advice.

Foundation and voluntary-aided schools

- The employee must be given a right to a **personal hearing** by the staff dismissal committee before the decision is made;
- s/he must be given an opportunity to **appeal** against the decision to the dismissal appeal committee before the governors give effect to it by issuing a notice of dismissal;
- the **headteacher** is **entitled to attend** any hearing or meeting to give advice;
- where the **CEO** of the LEA has been given **advisory rights**, s/he (or a representative) is entitled to attend any hearing or meeting to give advice. Where – in the case of the VA church school – the CEO has these rights, the appropriate diocesan officer has the same entitlement to attend and advise.

These safeguards apply irrespective of the grounds for the proposed dismissal – whether it is by reason of conduct, capability, health or redundancy – and irrespective of the employee's length of service. However, the Schedules of the SSFA 1998 provide that the hearing and appeal rights **only** apply to staff on **fixed-term contracts** if they have been continuously employed at the school for at least **one year**. Further, these rights do not apply to teachers barred from teaching by the Secretary of State or the General Teaching Council, nor to newly-qualified teachers who fail their induction period (SSFA 1998, Schedules 16 and 17).

A case heard by the Employment Appeal Tribunal (EAT) in 1999 confirmed the importance of these hearing rights, and how they must operate. An LEA school in Devon attempted to have a dismissal notice issued to a teacher before her appeal had been heard. The EAT ruled that this contravened the requirements of the SSFA 1998. These entitled her to 'an opportunity to appeal' – ie to have her appeal heard – before any dismissal decision was implemented (**Howard -v- Brixington Infants School and Devon County Council** – see Chapter 15).

The legislation does not set out explicit rules as to the conduct of these hearings, apart from specifying that the membership of an **appeal committee** must include at least the same number of governors as the staff dismissal committee which made the original decision – and that no member of the original committee can sit to hear the appeal (Regulation 47). ATL's strong advice (in conformity with ACAS guidance) is that employees should:

- be given reasonable **notice** of any hearing or appeal (at least five working days);
- be given clear **written details** of the

complaints and/or reasons for their proposed dismissal;

■ be entitled to **bring a representative**.

The Employment Relations Act 1999 will in due course give employees the legal right to be accompanied at disciplinary or dismissal hearings.

In co-ordination with the placing of dismissal decisions in the hands of governors, employment legislation provides that any complaint of **unfair dismissal** by a member of the school staff is pursued **against the governing body** (rather than against the LEA, who may be the formal employer).

The involvement of employee governors

There is no general restriction on teacher or staff governors – or other governors who happen to be employees – taking part in disciplinary, dismissal or appeal decisions in schools.

Needless to say, however, such governors must not participate if they have a pecuniary interest in the outcome (eg if they could be a candidate for a vacancy that would arise from a dismissal – see Chapter 15) or if they were directly involved in the incidents or complaints under consideration.

But, subject to those provisos, they are as eligible as any other governor to sit on a staff dismissal or appeal committee. Nonetheless, when appointing members to these committees, the governing body may decide against selecting employee governors. Moreover, school governors who are also employees may understandably feel reluctant to 'sit in judgement' on their colleagues.

13   POWERS OF INTERVENTION

With the implementation of the 1998 School Standards and Framework Act (the SSFA 1998) in September 1999, the Government has brought together the various powers vested in LEAs and the Secretary of State so that they now apply equally to all maintained schools: community, VC, VA, foundation and special. The powers (and the procedures for exercising them) are set out in detail in **DfEE Circular 6/99: Schools Causing Concern.** However, the key points are as follows:

LEA POWERS

The maintaining local authority has four intervention powers, exercisable in defined sets of circumstances. Broadly speaking, these are designed to provide an 'escalating' response to serious difficulties over standards of education, school management or breakdowns in discipline.

THE CODE OF PRACTICE ON LEA-SCHOOL RELATIONS

Valuable guidance on the use of these powers by local authorities is contained in the DfEE's statutory **Code of Practice on**

LEA-School Relations 1999. This confirms that schools should be given the maximum possible discretion to make decisions for themselves and that 'unnecessary intervention is not merely wasteful of resources and distracting for schools, but can undermine the school's sense of ownership for the standards it achieves'. Intervention should be very much the exception rather than the rule.

Further, the Code makes clear that the use of intervention powers should never come as a surprise to the governors or the headteacher. 'A written explanation should always be given to the governing body and headteacher detailing the LEA's concern and the evidence on which the LEA is relying. The school should be given an opportunity to respond and state its view'. In effect, therefor, the LEA should observe the principles of natural justice in considering intervention. In particular, any action taken by the LEA should:

- ■ be **proportionate** to the problem;
- ■ treat schools in all categories **consistently**;
- ■ never be influenced by **whether the school chooses to use LEA services**.

The four specific intervention powers are as follows:

Formal warning notice

- ■ firstly, the LEA may issue a **formal warning notice** to a governing body (Section 15, SSFA 1998). The triggers for this are either:
  - – **that the standards of pupils' performance are unacceptably low** (and likely to remain so); and/or
  - – a **'serious breakdown in the way the school is managed or governed'** such

as to prejudice pupils' standards of performance; and/or
  - – a **threat to the safety** of pupils or staff (whether by a breakdown of discipline or otherwise).

The LEA must, before issuing the notice, have informed the school of the concerns and given it reasonable time to remedy them. The notice gives the governing body further time to remedy the difficulties (the 'compliance period'). If the governing body fails to comply, the LEA may then invoke one or more of its further powers:

Appointing additional governors

- ■ secondly, it may appoint **additional governors** to the school. No specific limit is set on the number that can be added. This power is exercisable in any of three circumstances (Section 16, SSFA 1998):
  - – if the governing body has failed to remedy the issues raised in an LEA's **warning notice** within the 'compliance period';
  - – if an OFSTED report identifies **'serious weaknesses'** in one or more areas of its activities;
  - – if an OFSTED report states that the school requires **'special measures'** (ie it is **'failing** or likely to fail to give its pupils an **acceptable standard of education'**);

Suspending the delegated budget

- ■ thirdly, the local authority can **suspend the school's delegated budget**. This power can arise in any of five circumstances (Sections 17 and 51 and Schedule 15, SSFA 1998):

– if the governing body has failed (as above) to remedy the issues raised in the LEA's **warning notice** within the compliance period; or

– if an OFSTED report identifies **serious weaknesses** (see above); or

– if an OFSTED report calls for **'special measures'** (see above); or

– if the governing body has been 'guilty of a **substantial or persistent failure'** to comply with any delegation requirement or restriction; or

– if the governors are **not managing the budget in a satisfactory manner**.

Before suspending the delegation, the LEA must – unless there is gross incompetence or another emergency – give the governing body at least one month's notice, setting out the reasons. The local authority must **review** any suspension which has been in force for at least two months before the beginning of each financial year.

In the case of the last two circumstances above, the governors may **appeal** to the Secretary of State against the imposition of a suspension of their budget – or a refusal to revoke it following a review.

If, following a **formal warning**, the LEA is proposing to appoint additional governors or suspend the delegated budget, it must do so within two months of the end of the compliance period. Before taking either of these steps, the LEA must inform the headteacher and governors in writing of its intention.

Where the school is in the **'special measures'** category above, the LEA can appoint additional governors or suspend the delegated budget **only** if the Secretary of State declines to use her/his powers to do so (see below). Ten days must elapse from the DfEE's receipt of the LEA's 'action plan' (produced in response to the OFSTED report) before the LEA takes either of these initiatives in order to enable the Minister to decide whether to act. If s/he does not do so, the authority can then intervene.

DfEE Circular 6/99 emphasises that LEAs should not, under the formal warning notice procedure above, exercise their powers to appoint governors or withdraw the budget unless these are judged appropriate measures in the circumstances – taking account of any efforts or progress the school is making and the reasons for any failures.

Breakdown of discipline

The fourth LEA power is:

■ to take 'such steps as they consider are required' – including **giving directions** to the governing body and/or headteacher – to prevent or remedy a **breakdown of discipline** at the school (Section 62, SSFA 1998). This intervention can be triggered in two ways: either following a **formal warning** from the LEA as to a threat to **safety** or, alternatively, where the **behaviour** of pupils or actions taken by them (or their parents) is – or is about to be – **severely prejudicing education**. In this latter case, the authority must **inform** the governors before taking action.

The **Code of Practice on LEA-School Relations** emphasises that this is a 'reserve power of last resort', to be used only to create 'an opportunity in which constructive action can be taken to resolve an immediate problem and ensure it cannot recur'.

THE SECRETARY OF STATE'S POWERS

The Minister's powers arise only where a school has been assessed in an OFSTED report as requiring **special measures** (ie 'is failing, or likely to fail, to give its pupils an acceptable standard of education'). In these circumstances, s/he may take either of two initiatives (Sections 18 and 19, SSFA 1998):

Appointing additional governors

■ firstly, the Secretary of State may appoint **additional governors** (again, no specific limit is set on the number who can be added). This power overrides the LEA's capacity to appoint additional governors (see above). Furthermore, the Secretary of State may appoint one of these governors as **chair**, can provide for the appointees to be **paid** allowances and/or remuneration, and can set their **term of office** to be shorter or longer than the customary four years. Before appointing governors, the Minister will consult the governing body (and, in the case of a voluntary school, the appropriate diocesan authority) as to the skills and expertise required. Where the Secretary of State appoints additional governors, the LEA cannot suspend the delegated budget. If the authority has already done so, the Minister will, at the governing body's request, revoke the suspension.

Directing closure

■ secondly, the Minister can **direct the school's closure** at a given date. Although this could be implemented at any time, DfEE Circular 6/99 confirms that the Secretary of State will normally allow a school and its LEA time – typically two years – to implement any recovery plans which have been agreed with the Inspectorate. If a school has been failing for more than two years with no imminent date for removal from special measures, the Secretary of State will consider using this power to direct closure if the LEA is unwilling to do so. The normal statutory consultations are not required for such a closure. However, before giving a closure direction, the Minister must consult the governing body and the LEA (and also, in the case of a foundation or voluntary school provided by a church, the appropriate diocesan authority). If, following consultation, s/he decides to direct closure, the Secretary of State will give written notice to the LEA, the governing body, the headteacher and any other consultees.

THE DIOCESAN AUTHORITIES' POWERS

Where an LEA appoints additional governors to a **voluntary-aided** (VA) school under the **'serious weaknesses'** or **'formal warning notice'** procedures above, the appropriate diocese may also appoint an equivalent number of **additional foundation governors** (Section 16, SSFA 1998). They will have the same term of office as the LEA-appointed governors.

In the case of a VA school requiring **special measures**, the diocese can (if the Minister does **not** utilise the power to appoint governors within the ten-day period described above) take the initiative to appoint an unlimited number of **additional foundation governors**. This is irrespective of whether the LEA is exercising its powers to appoint further governors. However, where the Secretary of State **does** appoint additional governors to a VA school under special measures, there is no parallel right for the diocese to appoint an equivalent number of additional governors.

14 CONFLICTS OF INTEREST – WITHDRAWALS

All governors are entitled to play a full and active part in the decisions of the governing body. However, there are certain circumstances where governors must **withdraw** from a governing body or committee meeting – normally because they have a **conflict of interest,** ie they might gain personally or financially from the decision under consideration.

Helpfully, the 1999 School Government Regulations ('the 1999 Regulations') deal with many of these situations in some detail. However, they also contain new provisions on withdrawal which are not clearly defined. ATL hopes that this guidance will help clarify how the provisions should operate in practice and will assist in avoiding disputes.

Regulation 57 and Schedule 6 set out the current rules (see Appendix B of this document). There are now two situations in which members – either at a full governing body meeting or a committee – **must withdraw.** These are :

■ where there may be a **conflict of interest,** ie a conflict between the interests of the individual and her/his duty as a governor or a member of a committee; or

■ where a **fair hearing** is required and there is 'any **reasonable doubt**' about an individual's **'ability to act impartially'** in relation to any matter under consideration.

In such circumstances, the member must **disclose** the interest, **withdraw** from the meeting while the item of business in question is being discussed, and **not vote** upon it. The individual may, however, attend for the purpose of **giving evidence** at a hearing or (where appropriate) making **representations**.

For obvious reasons, the Regulations prevent a governor from participating in decisions on her/his appointment or removal – whether as a governor, member of a committee, chair, vice-chair or as clerk – or on the admission or exclusion of her/his own child. In a similar way, a governor who has made allegations, or has been a witness to incidents which are the subject of disciplinary proceedings, cannot take part in any consideration of the case. These restrictions apply equally to the headteacher in her/his role as governor. Therefor, in discussion of a disciplinary case in which the head has had prior involvement, s/he may attend the governors' meeting as headteacher, but cannot consider or vote on the outcome as a governor.

The Regulation makes clear that a person should not be required to withdraw merely because the issue under consideration affects another school of which s/he happens to be a governor or committee member. Furthermore, if the person concerned is the **clerk**, s/he can remain in the meeting as clerk and must withdraw only if her/his pay or disciplinary action against her/him is under consideration.

Where a dispute arises as to whether a person must withdraw, Regulation 57(6) now provides that this will be decided by the other members of the governing body (or committee) present.

CONFLICTS OF INTEREST

Interests can be either **personal** (for example, where the admission or exclusion of the governor's own child is under consideration) or – more frequently – financial or '**pecuniary**' (for instance, where the individual stands to profit from a contract or appointment being discussed). Similarly, an interest can be **direct** or **indirect**.

Schedule 6 provides some significant detail on how the rules must be applied generally and as to particular situations:

■ an **indirect interest** arises if the individual (or her/his nominee) is an employee, partner or member of an undertaking which either has a direct pecuniary interest in, or is itself, the business with which a contract is being contemplated. However, employment by, or membership of, a public body does not count here. Note that an indirect interest does not mean a potential or contingent interest. Therefor, a governor or committee

member does not have to withdraw merely because s/he might in future acquire an interest (see also page 52 below);

■ the rules on disclosure and withdrawal operate when a **relative living with** the individual has, to her/his knowledge, an interest in the issue under discussion. 'Relative' here is defined to include a spouse and a partner living with a person 'as if s/he were that person's spouse';

■ **employee governors** are obliged to withdraw and not vote on any consideration of a particular **individual's pay or performance appraisal.** This does not apply to the headteacher, who can participate in these matters for all other staff – but not her or his own pay or performance appraisal;

■ governors and committee members are not precluded from discussing or voting on proposals to take out **insurance cover** merely because they have a pecuniary interest in the issue;

■ a governor (or committee member) is not prevented from **entering a contract** with the governing body – provided s/he complies with the rules on disclosure of the interest and withdraws from discussion of the issue;

■ an interest does **not** arise for an employee (including the headteacher):

  – where her/his only interest is **no greater than the generality** of other staff;

  – just because the matter under consideration is the school's **curriculum**; or

  – just because the issue **involves expenditure** by the governing body.

As a result, teacher and staff governors are perfectly entitled to vote on, for example, proposals to redecorate the staffroom, to introduce mixed-ability teaching, or to apply a general freeze on vacancies. Similarly, they are not precluded by these rules from discussion of the school's redundancy procedure, its general pay policy, or from participation in the appointment process. It is only when the focus shifts to the position of **individuals** – be it their appointment, promotion, dismissal or (most specifically) pay/performance appraisal – that considerations of a conflict of interest may, or will, apply.

Helpful guidance on how the rules on pecuniary interest are to be applied here was given by two cases in 1989. Questions arose as to whether the teacher governors at LEA schools had a pecuniary interest in proposals for their schools to change status, on the basis that the potential new school might enhance (or worsen) the teachers' conditions of service. One case concerned a proposal to become grant-maintained, the other a conversion to a city technology college (CTC).

In **Bostock -v- Kay**, the Court of Appeal decided that the teacher governors could not take part in the governors' decision on conversion to a **CTC** because there was a real prospect of financial gain. However, when the question was consideration of GM status, the same Court decided, in **R -v- The Governors of Small Heath School,** that the teacher governors did not have a pecuniary interest in whether the school became **grant-maintained**. As the judge put it: 'In the present case there was no evidence to show that the position of the four (employed) governors was likely to alter'.

A full discussion of these cases is included in chapter 15.

ABILITY TO ACT IMPARTIALLY IN HEARINGS

The 1999 Regulations introduce a new requirement for governors (and committee members) to withdraw. This is 'where a **fair hearing** is required and there is any **reasonable doubt** about the relevant person's **ability to act impartially** in relation to any matter' (Regulation (54(2) – our emphasis).

Significantly, this new category for withdrawal applies only where a fair hearing is required. It appears clear that it arises only where the **position of an individual** is being decided at a formal **hearing**, ie a member of staff's dismissal (or appeal against it) or a pupil's admission or exclusion is under consideration. It does **not** apply to other issues, such as decisions on the budget, expenditure, educational matters, the future of the school or the appointment of staff.

Nevertheless, it is presently unclear how this will operate in practice – and the Regulations give no criteria for any assessment of an individual's ability to act impartially. This is a matter of concern.

For the present, ATL considers that there are three important issues to highlight here:

■ the new rule arises **only** in formal hearings of an individual's position – where there is a duty to act fairly;

■ it applies to **all governors equally.** The Regulation is not directed at (and must not be used to 'target') any particular category of governor – such as elected governors. For example, it does not disentitle employed governors from sitting on appointment, dismissal or appeal committees. It must not be suggested that staff are in some way automatically unable to act impartially on such issues;

■ the rule must not be invoked for the purpose of curtailing discussion or preventing the expression of robust (and perhaps unwelcome) opinions. Governors are entitled to express forthright, sincerely-held views. In short, the Regulation **must not be utilised to stifle debate.**

Accordingly, ATL considers that – in the absence of a personal or pecuniary interest in a matter under consideration – the governing body should be very cautious in calling on members to withdraw because of an apparent inability to act impartially. **Clear reasons** should be given in any individual case. Circumstances in which it will be appropriate to invoke this provision will, we believe, be rare.

APPOINTMENT PANELS

Perhaps the most contentious area, as far as conflicts of interest are concerned, is participation in appointments. Although teacher and staff governors have no **entitlement** to be selected for an appointment panel (or any other governors' committee, for that matter) there is no general restriction upon their taking part. In many cases, they are perfectly eligible to participate in appointments – subject to the rules on pecuniary interests.

Noble -v- ILEA, a leading case brought in 1982 under the School Government

Regulations then current (which included somewhat different wording), established how these rules generally operate. Mr Kazakos, the teacher governor, participated in a governors' appointment panel which promoted an internal applicant to the post of deputy. He subsequently applied for the vacancy that he had helped to create. The Court of Appeal held that his involvement breached the Regulations, and decided to overturn the appointment. The selection process had to be undertaken afresh. Significantly, Mr Kazakos was still allowed to take part in this second selection procedure, but only after he undertook not to apply for the vacancy if the internal applicant were to be appointed again. (This case is discussed in more detail in Chapter 15.)

This clearly implies that even a governor who is a potential candidate for a contingent vacancy can still participate in a selection panel, provided s/he formally agrees not to seek to benefit from it. The position may be summarised thus:

■ An employee governor who considers that s/he will be (or has not ruled out the possibility that s/he might be) a candidate for a vacancy created by the promotion, retirement, demotion or dismissal of an existing member of staff should declare an interest and withdraw from any consideration of, or any vote upon, the matter.

■ An employee governor who undertakes not to apply for a vacancy which may arise from the promotion (or demotion) of a member of staff, and formally indicates that s/he would not accept the appointment if offered, has explicitly abandoned any potential interest in the process and may therefor participate in discussion of, and any vote on, the matter.

Consider, however, a further possibility. A governing body intends to fill a vacancy for which there is an internal candidate, Mrs Firstrate. If she is appointed, there could be a chain reaction, ie the consequential possibility that another teacher at the school, Mr Gogetter, will be appointed to the resulting vacancy. Should the teacher governor Ms Hopeful be required to withdraw from any discussion and vote(s) upon the vacancy for which Mrs Firstrate is a candidate? Do the rules of pecuniary interest operate with a 'domino effect'? ATL considers that they do not.

Even though the Regulation calls for withdrawal where 'there may be a conflict of interest', ATL does not believe that a governor should be required to withdraw from discussion or a vote simply because there is a remote possibility that s/he might, as events unfold, come to have an interest in their outcome.

The conclusion is that the rules restricting teacher and staff governors' involvement in governing body decisions relate to highly specific circumstances. The occasions on which they must withdraw are, in practice, relatively rare. Accordingly, employee governors (and other governors, for that matter) should guard against being persuaded or intimidated into non-participation. In the vast majority of issues, the teacher and staff governors' views are entitled to exactly the same expression and weight as those of their governor colleagues.

15 SIGNIFICANT CASE LAW

THE REMOVAL OF GOVERNORS

The independence of appointed governors

Two cases have a direct bearing upon the role of appointed governors:

R -v- ILEA ex parte Brunyate

([1989] 1 WLR 542, House of Lords)

In this case, the Inner London Education Authority removed two of its own appointed governors from two voluntary-controlled (VC) schools because they **refused to vote** in accordance **with the authority's wishes** as to the future of the schools. This was held by the House of Lords to be a usurpation of the governors' independent function, and an **unlawful exercise of the power of removal** (then under Section 21 of the Education Act 1944).

R -v- Westminster Roman Catholic Diocese Trustee ex parte Andrews

([1990] COD 25, Court of Appeal)

In a complementary decision, the Court of Appeal held that the trustee of a voluntary-aided (VA) school **cannot remove** an appointed governor on the grounds that the governor **refuses to support a scheme**, proposed by the trustee, which would change the character of the school. Lord Justice Glidewell concluded that the control of the characteristics of the school, and the nature of the education provided, were a matter exclusively for the governors. It was not a matter over which the trustee had control.

The significance of these cases is discussed in more detail in Chapter 7, page 23. They make clear that – although appointing bodies can remove appointed governors – they cannot do so for an **improper motive**.

Removals for 'political balance'

R -v- Warwickshire County Council ex parte Dill-Russell
([1989] LGR 640, Court of Appeal) (see also page 24)

Mrs Dill-Russell was a Liberal Democrat-nominated LEA governor of a special school in Warwickshire. In May 1989, the local government elections resulted in control of the County Council passing to the Conservatives. Although there were no complaints against her personally, the incoming council administration proposed to remove Mrs Dill-Russell, replacing her with a Conservative nominee. She objected – pointing to the earlier rulings (outlined above) as to the independence of governors. However, the Court of Appeal upheld her removal. It was held **legitimate for a local authority to remove appointed governors to reflect the changed political complexion of the council**.

Natural justice in removing governors

R -v- Brent LBC ex parte Assegai
([1987], 151 LG Rev 891, High Court) (see also page 23)

Dr Kuba Assegai was a governor appointed by the London Borough of Brent. He was (in the judge's words) 'a large, colourful and exuberant personality' who would express his views forcefully. Relations became seriously strained and, after several incidents (which culminated in Dr Assegai physically threatening the chair of the Education Committee), the authority finally – in 1987 – decided to remove him forthwith. He challenged this in the High Court.

The judge quashed his removal – not because it was unreasonable – but because **the rules of natural justice had not been observed**. Dr Assegai had been given no notice of the intended decision, nor any opportunity to state his case before it was made.

PECUNIARY INTEREST

The appointment of staff

Noble -v- ILEA
(82 Knight's Local Government Reports 291, Court of Appeal)

In this case (decided under the School Government Regulations in force at that time), Mr Kazakos, a teacher governor, took part in a governors' appointment panel to select a deputy headteacher.

The panel decided by one vote to appoint the internal candidate, Mr Noble. Mr Kazakos subsequently applied for the vacancy created by Mr Noble's promotion. It appeared clear that Mr Kazakos had a pecuniary interest in the selection process. The unsuccessful external applicant for the post of deputy (Mrs Gadd) objected, and issued proceedings claiming that the teacher governor's participation invalidated Mr Noble's appointment.

The Court of Appeal held that Mr Kazakos, having an interest, **should not have participated** in the procedure by which Mr Noble was selected. **His appointment was therefor nullified.** The Court of Appeal disallowed Mr Noble's appeal that, having been offered the post and having accepted it, he should be confirmed in it. The Court endorsed the authority's decision to re-run the appointment process – which in fact resulted in Mrs Gadd being appointed to the post.

Although the case pre-dates the current School Government Regulations, one of its key features may have considerable significance for present practice. At the second governors' meeting (which led to the selection of the external candidate, Mrs Gadd), Mr Kazakos was allowed to participate and to vote **because he had undertaken not to apply for the post that would become vacant if Mr Noble were once again selected**. Although it was not necessary for the Court of Appeal to decide the point, it offered no criticism of Mr Kazakos' participation in the second election process.

The factor which flawed Mr Noble's initial selection was not that Mr Kazakos participated in the vote, but that he subsequently applied for the vacancy thus created, so revealing an interest which should have been declared at the outset.

The implication is that Mr Kazakos, having made clear at the second governors' meeting that he would not apply for any vacancy arising from its decision, had renounced – and extinguished – the interest he previously had. He was therefor now entitled to participate in the appointment process.

Conflicts of interest are discussed in detail in Chapter 14.

Proposals for schools to change status

Two cases have been reported on this issue, with contrasting outcomes in two different circumstances:

Bostock and others -v- Kay and others
([1989] 133S J749, Court of Appeal)

Here, the Court of Appeal upheld a ruling **that the teacher governors of schools considering whether or not to become city technology colleges (CTCs) must not participate in any discussion of the issue or vote on any question concerning it at governors' meetings**.

It was decided that a pecuniary interest arose in the prospect of the teachers receiving a higher salary if they were employed at the proposed new CTCs, or receiving redundancy payments if they were not so employed.

In dismissing the teacher governors' appeal (pursued on the grounds that the interest was too remote to be taken into account), Lord Justice Glidewell accepted the lower court's finding that 'any teacher invited to vote on the proposal would understandably be tempted at the very least to ask how it would affect him financially; he would therefor have a financial interest in the adoption of the proposal'.

Regina -v- The Governors of Small Heath School ex parte Birmingham City Council
([1990] COD 23, Court of Appeal)

In this second case, the issue was the participation of governors who were employees in a school's consideration of grant-maintained status.

The Court of Appeal ruled that these governors did **not** have a pecuniary interest. Lord Justice Glidewell (who had also presided over the decision in **Bostock -v- Kay** above, which dealt with a proposal for a school to become a CTC) made a clear distinction between the two cases as follows:

> 'The main difference stemmed from the difference between a grant-maintained school and a CTC. The only necessary changes when a county school became a GM school were that the cost of the school's financial support was transferred from the local education authority to the Secretary of State and that the governors gained greater autonomy. The school itself did not need to alter at all.
>
> 'The change to a CTC was much more fundamental, the old school ceasing to exist and being replaced by a completely new institution at which the curriculum might change and where the existing staff might, or might not, be engaged.'

The Court of Appeal concluded, therefor, that the evidence did not establish that any of these governors had a pecuniary interest in the school becoming grant-maintained.

THE APPOINTMENT OF STAFF

Regina -v- Birmingham City Council ex parte McKenna
(Times Law Report 16.5.91, High Court)

Mrs McKenna applied for the headship of a Birmingham LEA primary school. In accordance with the requirements of the legislation, the governing body appointed a six-member panel to make a recommendation. The panel was to meet three times: to prepare a 'long list'; to interview the long list candidates; and, finally, to interview the shortlisted applicants. However, the panel scheduled its second meeting for a date on which it was known that one governor could not be present. It decided to proceed with only five members.

Mrs McKenna, who was not selected for the shortlist at this second meeting, brought a claim that the panel's proceedings were flawed and therefor unlawful. The authority argued in response that the panel (as an effective committee of the governing body) could govern its own proceedings. The judge held that the appointment process for a headteacher vacancy, being set down in statute, must be followed closely. In this instance, the panel was not entitled to sit without a full complement of members, and had acted improperly.

However, in the circumstances of the case, the Court declined to exercise its discretion to overturn the panel's decision, considering that no injustice had in fact been done.

Although Mrs McKenna's claim did not succeed, this case underlines the importance of school selection panels (and particularly those considering the appointment of heads or deputies) observing the statutory requirements strictly. The legislative controls on governors' appointments of staff are explained in Chapter 11.

THE DISMISSAL OF STAFF

Howard -v- Brixington Infants School and Devon County Council
(IDS Brief 638, June 1999, EAT)

Ms Howard was a teacher employed by the LEA at an infants' school. Following a theft at the school, she was summoned to a governors' hearing which resolved to dismiss her without notice. Her union informed the governors of her intention to appeal, but the governing body proceeded to arrange for notice of dismissal to be issued straight away. Her subsequent appeal was not upheld.

The teacher claimed unfair dismissal, challenging the procedure which had implemented her dismissal before her appeal had been heard (contrary to the requirements of the legislation). The employers responded that they had formally delegated power to dismiss from the LEA to the governing body and that, in any event, the Schedule (see Chapter 12) merely required the employee to be given 'an opportunity to appeal' before the dismissal was implemented – it did not explicitly require the appeal to be heard.

Ms Howard succeeded on both issues. The Employment Appeal Tribunal ruled that the LEA cannot delegate its duties to governing bodies in such cases. The governors have the responsibility of conducting the hearing and any appeal, and then notifying the LEA to issue the notice of dismissal. More significantly, the case decided that the **appeal must be heard before the LEA is notified of the decision and notice is given (and, by implication, that the employee must continue to receive salary meanwhile)**.

EMPLOYERS' RIGHT TO REFUSE PERMISSION TO EMPLOYEES TO SERVE AS GOVERNORS

Champion -v- Chief Constable of Gwent
([1990] 1 WLR 1, House of Lords)
In this case, a police constable successfully appealed against his Chief Constable's instruction that he should not serve as a parent governor.

The House of Lords rejected suggestions that a disappointed candidate for a teaching post might think that a police offer who was a governor would unfairly use information gained through his work to prevent an appointment, or that members of the police force should not be involved in 'controversial decisions'.

16 USEFUL FURTHER READING

- Advisory Centre for Education:
  Governors' Handbook 1998

- Croner Publications:
  School Governors' Manual

- Croner Publications:
  The Heads' Legal Guide

- DfEE:
  Circular 15/98 **New Framework Governing Bodies** 1998

- DfEE:
  Circular 6/99 **Schools Causing Concern** 1999

- DfEE:
  School Governors – A Guide to the Law

- DfEE:
  Guidance on Good Governance 1996

- DfEE:
  Code of Practice on LEA-School Relations 1999

- Electoral Reform Ballot Services:
  How to Run an Election by Single Transferable Vote

- House of Commons Education and Employment Committee Report:
  The Role of School Governors July 1999

- Sallis, J:
  School Governors: A Question and Answer Guide 1995 *(Butterworth Heinemann)*

- Sallis, J:
  Managing Better with Governors 1999 *(Financial Times/Pitman Publishing)*

17 HELPFUL ORGANISATIONS

(Please note that new standard dialling codes have been used for telephone numbers)

Advisory Centre for Education (ACE)
1B Aberdeen Studios
22 Highbury Grove
London N5 2DQ
020 7354 8321 (advice line)
020 7354 8318 (business line)

Campaign for State Education (CASE)
158 Durham Road
London SW20 0DG
020 8944 8206

Department for Education and Employment (DfEE)
Sanctuary Buildings
Great Smith Street
Westminster
London SW1P 3BT
020 7925 5000

The Education Network
22 Upper Woburn Place
London WC1H 0TB
020 7490 4942

National Association of Governors and Managers (NAGM)
Suite 36/38
21 Bennetts Hill
Birmingham B2 5QP
0121 643 5787

National Confederation of Parent-Teacher Associations (NCPTA)
2 Ebbsfleet Industrial Estate
Stonebridge Road
Gravesend
Kent DA11 9DZ
01474 560 618

APPENDIX A: THE NEW CONSTITUTIONS OF GOVERNING BODIES

The revised compositions of governing bodies from 1 September 1999 for the new categories of maintained schools are set out in DfEE Circular 15/98: **New Framework Governing Bodies** and in the Education (School Government – Transition to New Framework) Regulations 1998, SI 1998 No 2763. In many cases, governing bodies have been given some flexibility to choose the size of constitution which suits their school. The membership requirements and options, in concise form, are set out below. Note that, where the governing body is able to choose a constitution from a range of options, it must select one of the columns for which it is eligible – it cannot 'mix and match' between the columns.

(The figures in brackets in the tables offer a rough-and-ready comparison with the typical former composition in place before September 1999):

Community school constitutions

Governor category	Secondary		Primary			
	a	b	c	d	e	f
Parent	6(5)	5(4)	5(4)	4(3)	3(3)	3(2)
LEA	5(5)	4(4)	4(4)	3(3)	2(3)	2(2)
Teacher	2(2)	2(1 or 2)	2(2)	1(1)	1(1)	1(1)
Staff	1(-)	1(-)	1(-)	1(-)	1(-)	0(-)
Co-opted	5(6)	4(4 or 5)	4(5)	3(4)	2(4)	2(3)
Head*	1(1)	1(1)	1(1)	1(1)	1(1)	1(1)
Total	20(19)	17(14 or 16)	17(16)	13(12)	10(12)	10(9)

* The headteacher may elect not to be a governor.

Community **secondary** schools with 600 or more pupils **must** take column a.
Community secondaries with under 600 pupils may choose columns a or b.
Community **primaries** with 100 or more pupils may choose columns c or d.
Community primaries with under 100 pupils may choose columns c, d, e or f.

Primaries serving one or more **minor authorities** (parish, community or district councils) **must** co-opt an **additional governor** nominated by the authority/authorities.

Schools with a **sponsor** – ie a body or person giving substantial (voluntary) financial assistance – **may** choose one or two additional co-opted governors nominated by the sponsor(s). These co-options replace the former category of 'sponsor governor'.

If the school is in an **Education Action Zone** (EAZ), the governors **may choose** to have an additional co-opted governor nominated by the Education Action Forum.

Foundation school constitutions

Governor category	Secondary			Primary			
	a	b	c	d	e	f
Parent	7(5)	6(5)	6(5)	5(4 or 5)	4(4or 5)	4(4 or 5)
LEA	2(-)	2(-)	2(-)	2(-)	2(-)	2(-)
Teacher	2(1or 2)	2(1 or 2)	1(1 or 2)	1(1 or 2)	1(1 or 2)	1(1 or 2)
Staff	1(-)	1(-)	1(-)	1(-)	1(-)	0(-)
Foundation or Partnership	5(9)	4(8)	4(9)	3(7)	2(7)	2(5)
Co-opted	3(-)	2(-)	1(-)	1(-)	1(-)	1(-)
Head*	1(1)	1(1)	1(1)	1(1)	1(1)	1(1)
Total	21(17)	18(15)	16(17)	14(13)	12(13)	11(10)

(Partnership governors take the place of foundation governors where the school does not have a foundation or trustees.)

* The headteacher may elect not to be a governor.

Foundation **secondary** schools with 600 or more pupils **must** take column a.
Foundation secondaries with under 600 pupils may choose columns a or b.
Foundation **primary** schools with over 100 pupils may choose columns c or d.
Foundation primaries with under 100 pupils may choose columns c, d, e or f.

Foundation schools which have a **sponsor** (ie a body or person giving substantial (voluntary) financial assistance) **may choose** one or two **additional co-opted** governors nominated by the sponsor(s). These co-options replace the former category of 'sponsor governors'.

If the school is in an **EAZ**, the governors **may choose** to have an additional co-opted governor nominated by the Education Action Forum.

Voluntary-aided school constitutions

Governor category	Secondary			Primary			
	a	b	c	d	e	formerly
Parent	3	2	2	1	1	(1 or more)
LEA	2	1	2	1	1	(1 or more)
Teacher	2	2	1	1	1	(1 or 2)
Staff	1	1	1	1	0	-
Head*	1	1	1	1	1	(1)
Foundation+	12	9	9	7	6	(6 or more)
Total	21	16	16	12	10	(10 or more)

* The headteacher may elect not to be a governor.

+ The **foundation governors** must outnumber the others by a set figure: by three in column a and by two in other cases. Therefor, if the head chooses not to be a governor, or if there are additional co-opted governors (see below), the number of foundation governors must be adjusted accordingly. At least three of the foundation governors in column a – or two in the other columns – must be **parents** of pupils currently at the school.

VA **secondary** schools with 600 or more pupils **must** take column a.
VA secondaries with under 600 pupils may choose columns a or b.
VA **primary** schools with 100 or more pupils may choose columns c or d.
VA primaries with under 100 pupils may choose columns c, d or e.

Primaries serving one or more **minor authorities** (parish, community or district councils) **must** co-opt an **additional governor** nominated by the authority/authorities.

VA schools which have a **sponsor** (ie a body or person giving substantial (voluntary) financial assistance) **may choose** one or two additional co-opted governors nominated by the sponsor(s). These co-options replace the former category of 'sponsor governors'.

If the school is in an **EAZ**, the governors **may choose** to have an additional co-opted governor nominated by the Education Action Forum.

Voluntary-controlled school constitutions

Governor category	Secondary		Primary			
	a	b	c	d	e	f
Parent	6(5)	5(4)	5(4)	4(3)	3(3)	3(2)
LEA	4(5)	3(4)	3(4)	3(3)	2(3)	2(2)
Teacher	2(2)	2(2)	1(2)	1(1)	1(1)	1(1)
Staff	1(-)	1(-)	1(-)	1(-)	1(-)	0(-)
Foundation	5(4)	4(4)	4(4)	3(3)	2(3)	2(2)
Co-opted	2(2)	2(1)	1(1)	1(1)	1(1)	1(1)
Head*	1(1)	1(1)	1(1)	1(1)	1(1)	1(1)
Total	21(19)	18(16)	16(16)	14(12)	11(12)	10(9)

VC **secondary** schools with 600 or more pupils **must** take column a.

VC secondaries with under 600 pupils may choose columns a or b.

VC **primary** schools with 100 or more pupils may choose columns c or d.

VC primaries with under 100 pupils may choose columns c, d, e or f.

* The headteacher may elect not to be a governor.

VC primaries serving one or more **minor authorities** (parish, community or district councils) **must** co-opt one additional governor nominated by the authority/authorities.

Schools which have a **sponsor** (ie a body or person giving substantial (voluntary) financial assistance) **may choose** one or two additional co-opted governors nominated by the sponsor(s). These co-options replace the former category of 'sponsor governor'.

If the school is in an **EAZ**, the governors **may choose** to have an additional co-opted governor nominated by the Education Action Forum.

Special schools

Special schools now have the status of either **community special** or **foundation special** schools. Their previous constitutions were generally as for county schools (ie regulated according to the number of pupils). Their new constitutions are as follows:

COMMUNITY SPECIAL SCHOOLS

Governor category	a	b	c	d
Parent	5	4	3	3
LEA	4	3	2	2
Teacher	2	1	1	1
Staff	1	1	1	0
Co-opted	4	3	2	2
Head*	1	1	1	1
Total	17	13	10	9

These schools, whether secondary or primary, may choose columns a, b, c, or d.

* The headteacher may elect not to be a governor.

Where the school is in a **hospital**, a **'representative'** governor **must** be appointed in place of one of the co-options above. This governor will be nominated by either the Health Authority or the NHS Trust, as appropriate.

Where the school is **not** in a hospital, the LEA **may** designate an appropriate voluntary organisation concerned with the school to appoint a representative governor in place of one of the co-options above.

Foundation special schools

Governor category	a	b	c	d
Parent	6	5	4	4
LEA	2	2	2	2
Teacher	1	1	1	1
Staff	1	1	1	0
Partnership	4	3	2	2
Co-opted	1	1	1	1
Head*	1	1	1	1
Total	16	14	12	11

Again, these schools, whether secondary or primary, may choose columns a, b, c or d.

* The headteacher may elect not to be a governor.

In the case of both types of special school, where there is a **sponsor** (ie a person or body who gives substantial (voluntary) financial assistance), the school may **choose** to have one or two additional co-opted governors nominated by the sponsor. Similarly, if it is in an **EAZ**, the school **may choose** to have an additional co-opted governor nominated by the Education Action Forum.

Appendix B: The Education (School Government) (England) Regulations 1999 SI 1999 No 2163

STATUTORY INSTRUMENTS

1999 No 2163

EDUCATION, ENGLAND

The Education (School Government) (England) Regulations 1999

Made	28 July 1999
Laid before Parliament	30 July 1999
Coming into force	
All regulations except Regulations 22(1), 29(11) and 51(3)	1 September 1999
Regulations 22(1), 29(11) and 51(3)	1 April 2000

ARRANGEMENT OF REGULATIONS

PART I

INTRODUCTION

1 Citation, commencement and application
2 Interpretation
3 Interpretation of 'governing body'

PART II

INSTRUMENTS OF GOVERNMENT AND GOVERNING BODY COMPOSITION

4 Application
5 Copies of instruments of government
6 Additional co-opted governors
7 Representative governors
8 Substitute foundation governors
9 Appointment of parent and partnership governors
10 Notification of vacancies and appointments
11 Joint appointments
12 Elections
13 Surplus governors

PART III

QUALIFICATIONS AND TENURE OF OFFICE

14   Application and interpretation
15   Qualifications and disqualifications
16   Term of office
17   Resignation
18   Removal
19   Removal of governors by the governing body
20   Notice of resignation or removal

PART IV

CLERKS

21   Application and interpretation
22   Clerk to the governing body: restrictions
23   Appointment of the clerk to the governing body
24   Dismissal of the clerk
25   Appointment and dismissal of the clerk where the school does not have a delegated budget
26   First clerk to the temporary governing body
27   Clerking on transition to the permanent governing body

PART V

MEETINGS AND PROCEEDINGS OF GOVERNING BODIES

28   Interpretation
29   Chairman and vice-chairman of the governing body
30   Removal from office of the chairman of the governing body
31   Chairman and vice-chairman of temporary governing bodies
32   Right of the headteacher to attend meetings
33   Public access to meetings
34   Convening of meetings of the governing body
35   Rescission and variation of resolutions
36   Termination and adjournment of meetings
37   Quorum
38   Proceedings of the governing body
39   Minutes of meetings
40   Publication of minutes and papers
41   Delegation of functions
42   Restrictions on delegation
43   Delegation of functions to the chairman and vice-chairman in cases of urgency
44   Reporting to the governing body following the exercise of delegated functions

PART VI

COMMITTEES OF GOVERNING BODIES

45   Interpretation and application
46   Establishment and constitution of committees of the governing body
47   Staff dismissal committee and dismissal appeal committee
48   Pupil discipline committee
49   Admissions committee
50   Disqualification of members of governing body committees
51   Clerks to committees
52   Meetings of committees
53   Proceedings of committees
54   Minutes of meetings of committees
55   Publication of minutes and papers of committees
56   Access to committee meetings

PART VII

57 RESTRICTIONS ON PERSONS TAKING PART IN PROCEEDINGS

PART VIII

58 TRANSITIONAL PROVISIONS

SCHEDULES

Schedule 1: Additional co-opted governors
Schedule 2: Parent governors
Schedule 3: Partnership governors
Schedule 4: Elections
Schedule 5: Qualifications and disqualifications
Schedule 6: Restrictions on persons taking part in proceedings of the governing body or their committees
Schedule 7: Transitional provisions

In exercise of the powers conferred on the Secretary of State by Sections 44(5) and (6), 138(7) and (8), and 144 of, and paragraphs 4, 5, 15(1) and (2), 16 and 17 of Schedule 9, paragraph 1 of Schedule 10, paragraphs 1 to 5 and 8 of Schedule 11 and paragraphs 4 and 5 of Schedule 12 to, the School Standards and Framework Act 1998(a) and all other enabling powers, the Secretary of State for Education and Employment hereby makes the following Regulations:

PART I

INTRODUCTION

Citation, commencement and application

1   (1)   These Regulations may be cited as the Education (School Government) (England) Regulations 1999.

(2)   These Regulations shall come into force on 1 September 1999, except for Regulations 22(1), 29(11) and 51 (3), which shall come into force on 1 April 2000.

(3)   These Regulations apply in relation to maintained schools and new schools in England.

(a)   1998 c 31; for the meaning of 'prescribed' and 'regulations' see section 142(1).

THE EDUCATION (SCHOOL GOVERNMENT) (ENGLAND) REGULATIONS 1999

Interpretation

2 (1) In these Regulations, unless the context otherwise requires:

'the 1996 Act' means the Education Act 1996**(b)**;

'the 1998 Act' means the School Standards and Framework Act 1998;

'additional co-opted governor' means a co-opted governor required by virtue of paragraph 15 of Schedule 9 to the 1998 Act;

'co-opted governor' includes an additional co-opted governor;

'employed to work' means employed under a contract of employment or a contract for services;

'employee of the local education authority' means a person employed by the local education authority in connection with their functions as a local education authority;

'the First Transitional Regulations' means the Education (School Government) (Transition to New Framework) Regulations 1998**(c)**;

'the headteacher', if there is more than one headteacher of the school in accordance with the Education (Head Teachers) Regulations 1999**(d)**, means any head teacher of the school;

'maintained school' means a community, community special, voluntary, foundation or foundation special school;

'new school' means a maintained school or proposed such school for which there is a temporary governing body constituted under Section 44 of the 1998 Act, a transitional governing body treated as so constituted by virtue of Regulation 13(5) of the Second Transitional Regulations, or a temporary governing body treated as so constituted by virtue of Regulation 13 of the School Organisation Regulations;

'School Organisation Regulations' means the Education (Transition to New Framework) (School Organisation Proposals) Regulations 1999**(e)**;

'the Second Transitional Regulations' means the Education (Transition to New Framework) (New Schools, Groups and Miscellaneous) Regulations 1999**(f)**;

'selection panel' means a selection panel for the appointment of headteachers or deputy headteachers constituted under paragraph 6 of Schedule 16 or paragraph 7 of Schedule 17 to the 1998 Act.

(2) Except where the context otherwise requires, the expressions used in these Regulations set out in the first column of the table below have the meaning given by (or, as the case may be) are to be interpreted in accordance with, the provisions referred to in the second column of that table:

'appropriate diocesan authority' (in relation to a Church of England or Roman Catholic Church school)	Section 142(1) and (4) of the 1998 Act;
'Education Action Forum'	Section 11(2) of the 1998 Act;
'education action zone'	Section 10(1) of the 1998 Act;
'have a delegated budget'	Section 49(7) of the 1998 Act;
'instrument of government'	Section 37(1) of the 1998 Act;
'representative governor'	paragraph 10 of Schedule 9 to the 1998 Act;
'school year'	Section 579(1) of the 1996 Act;

(b)   1996 c 56.
(c)   SI 1998/2763.
(d)   SI 1999/1287.
(e)   SI 1999/704.
(f)   SI 1999/362.

'temporary governing body' and 'temporary governors'	Section 44 of the 1998 Act, Regulation 13(5) of the Second Transitional Regulations and Regulation 13 of the School Organisation Regulations.

(3)   Unless the context otherwise requires, any reference in these Regulations to:

(a)   a numbered Part, Regulation or Schedule is a reference to the Part, Regulation or Schedule in these Regulations so numbered;

(b)   a numbered paragraph is a reference to the paragraph so numbered in the Regulation or Schedule in which the reference appears; and

(c)   a numbered sub-paragraph is a reference to the sub-paragraph so numbered in the paragraph in which the reference appears.

Interpretation of 'governing body'

3   Unless the context otherwise requires, any reference in these Regulations to the governing body, or the governing body of a school, is a reference to the governing body, or the governing body of a school, or temporary governing body (however constituted(a)) of any school or (as the case may be) new school to which the provision applies, and any reference to a governor is a reference to a member of such a governing body.

PART II

INSTRUMENTS OF GOVERNMENT AND GOVERNING BODY COMPOSITION

Application

4   Regulations 6 to 13 apply in relation to any maintained school conducted by an incorporated governing body constituted under an instrument of government (but not including a maintained school with a transitional governing body partly constituted under an instrument in accordance with Regulation 18(2) of the First Transitional Regulations)(b).

Copies of instruments of government

5   (1)   The local education authority which maintains or will maintain a school or a new school for which an instrument of government has been made shall secure that the persons set out in paragraph (2) are provided (free of charge) with:

(a)   a copy of the school's instrument of government; and

(b)   where any variation is made to the school's instrument of government

(i)   a copy of the order varying the instrument; and

(ii)   a consolidated version of the instrument of government incorporating all variations made by order of the local education authority (other than any variations which have ceased to have effect).

(2)   In relation to any school referred to in paragraph (1), the persons who are to be provided with the information referred to in paragraph (1)(a) and (b) are:

(i)   every member of the governing body of the school;

(ii)   every member of the temporary governing body of the school;

(iii)   any trustees under a trust deed relating to the school; and

(iv)   in the case of a Church of England or Roman Catholic Church school, the appropriate diocesan authority or, in the case of a new school which has not opened, the diocesan authority which will be the appropriate diocesan authority when the school opens.

(a)   See for the purposes of the composition of governing bodies on transition to the new schools framework, Regulations 18 and 19 of the First Transitional Regulations, regulations 13.30 and 49 of the Second Transitional Regulations and Regulation 13 of the School Organisation Regulations.

(b)   This Part should be read together with Schedules 9 and 12 to the 1998 Act. The constitution or reconstitution of the governing body under the first instrument of government made on transition for the new schools framework is dealt with in the First Transitional Regulations, or the Second Transitional Regulations.

THE EDUCATION (SCHOOL GOVERNMENT) (ENGLAND) REGULATIONS 1999

Additional co-opted governors

6 (1) Schedule 1 makes provision for the number of additional co-opted governors which may be required by the instrument of government for a maintained school by virtue of paragraph 15(1) and (2) of Schedule 9 to the 1998 Act, for the circumstances in which provision for such governors is authorised to be made, and for the categories of person from whom or from amongst whose members nominations for such appointments are to be sought.

(2) Subject to paragraph (3), if the governing body make or revoke a determination under paragraph 15(1) of Schedule 9 to the 1998 Act, the instrument of government shall be varied at the instance of the governing body in consequence**(a)**.

(3) Paragraph (2) does not apply where the governing body make or revoke a determination under paragraph 15(1) of Schedule 9 to the 1998 Act in anticipation of the replacement of the instrument of government on a change of category pursuant to Regulations under Schedule 8 to the 1998 Act.

Representative governors

7 (1) If there is any change in the body or bodies entitled to appoint a representative governor at a community special school (or in whether the school has a representative governor) by virtue of paragraph 10 of Schedule 9 to the 1998 Act, the instrument of government shall be varied at the instance of the governing body in consequence.

(2) Paragraph (1) does not apply if the change in question is related to a change of category (as referred to in Regulation 6(3)) and the instrument of government is to be replaced.

Substitute foundation governors

8 The instrument of government for a maintained school shall name the person or persons who shall be entitled to appoint a foundation governor to act in the place of an *ex officio* foundation governor in any case where:

(a) that *ex officio* foundation governor is unable or unwilling to act as such; or

(b) there is a vacancy in the office by virtue of which such a governorship exists.

Appointment of parent and partnership governors

9 (1) Schedule 2 sets out the circumstances in which parent governors required by the instrument of government shall be appointed by the governing body, and the requirements which must be complied with in relation to any such appointment**(b)**.

(2) Schedule 3 provides for the nomination and appointment of partnership governors required by the instrument of government.

Notification of vacancies and appointments

10 (1) Subject to paragraphs (2) and (3), where a vacancy in the office of an appointed member of the governing body arises, the clerk to the governing body shall as soon as is reasonably practicable give notice in writing of that fact to the person or persons entitled to appoint a person to that office.

(2) Subject to paragraph (3), the clerk to the governing body shall, at least two months before the date of the expiry of the term of office of an appointed member, give notice in writing of the expiry of that term to the person or persons entitled to appoint a person to that office.

(3) Paragraphs (1) and (2) shall not apply where the person or persons entitled to appoint a person to the office in question have already notified the clerk to the governing body in writing of the person appointed by them.

(a) The procedure for varying the instrument of government is in paragraph 4 of Schedule 12 to the 1998 Act.
(b) Generally parent governors are elected. See paragraph 4 of Schedule 9 to the 1998 Act.

(4) Where any person or persons make an appointment to the governing body, they shall give written notice of the appointment to the clerk to the governing body specifying the name and usual place of residence of the person so appointed.

(5) For the purposes of this regulation, 'appointed member' means:

(a) a foundation governor;

(b) an LEA governor;

(c) a co-opted governor;

(d) a representative governor; or

(e) a partnership governor.

Joint appointments

11 If:

(a) the instrument of government for a maintained school provides for one or more governors to be appointed by persons acting jointly, and

(b) those persons fail to make an agreed appointment,

the appointment shall be made by, or in accordance with a direction given by, the Secretary of State.

Elections

12 Schedule 4 makes provision for the election of governors.

Surplus governors

13 (1) Where:

(a) a maintained school has more governors of a particular category (other than foundation governors) **(a)** than are provided for by the instrument of government for the school in accordance with Part II of Schedule 9 to the 1998 Act, and

(b) the excess is not eliminated by the required number of governors of that category resigning,

such number of governors of that category as is required to eliminate the excess shall cease to hold office in accordance with paragraphs (2) and (3).

(2) The governors who are to cease to hold office shall be determined on the basis of seniority, the governor whose current period of continuous service (whether as a governor of one or more than one category) is the shortest being the first to cease to hold office.

(3) Where it is necessary for the purposes of paragraph (2) to select one or more governors from a group of equal seniority, it shall be done by drawing lots.

(4) For the purposes of this regulation, additional co-opted governors nominated by a particular category of person are treated as if they constituted a separate category of governor.

PART III

QUALIFICATIONS AND TENURE OF OFFICE

Application and interpretation

14 (1) This Part does not apply in relation to any member of a temporary governing body of a new school.

(2) In this Part, any reference to a governor continuing in office on transition to the new framework is a reference to a governor continuing in office under Regulation 13 of the First Transitional Regulations, Regulation 13 of the First Transitional Regulations as it applies by virtue of Regulation 20 of those Regulations, or Regulation 33 or 57 of the Second Transitional Regulations.

(a) Excess foundation governors are to be eliminated in accordance with the procedure set out in the instrument of government for the school.

Qualifications and disqualifications

15   Subject to Part VIII (transitional provisions), Schedule 5 sets out the circumstances in which a person is qualified or disqualified for holding or continuing in office, or for being elected, appointed or nominated, as a governor of a school.

Term of office

16   (1)   Subject to Part VIII (transitional provisions) and to paragraphs (2) to (6), any governor of a school required by an instrument of government and any additional governor or additional foundation governor appointed under Section 16(1) or (8) of the 1998 Act, shall hold office for a term of four years.

      (2)   Paragraph (1) shall not apply to any governor who is the headteacher of the school, or to any *ex officio* foundation governor.

      (3)   (a)   Any foundation governor appointed on or after 1 September 1999 (other than an additional foundation governor appointed under Section 16 of the 1998 Act or a substitute foundation governor) shall hold office for such term, not exceeding four years, as the person appointing him shall determine at the time of making the appointment and notify in writing to the clerk to the governing body of the school concerned at the time of notifying him of the appointment.

           (b)   In default of a term being determined and notified in accordance with sub-paragraph (a), a governor to whom that sub-paragraph applies shall hold office for a term of four years.

      (4)   Any co-opted governor (other than an additional co-opted governor) appointed for the purposes of the initial constitution of the permanent governing body of a new school under the first instrument of government shall hold office for the term of one year.

      (5)   For the purposes of this regulation, 'substitute governor' means any foundation governor appointed to act in the place of an *ex officio* foundation governor by virtue of any regulations made under paragraph 16 of Schedule 9 to the 1998 Act and 'the original governor' means the *ex officio* foundation governor in whose place the substitute governor is appointed to act.

      (6)   A substitute governor shall hold office until the earlier of the following:

           (a)   the expiry of four years from the date when his appointment takes effect;

           (b)   the date when the original governor gives written notice to the clerk to the governing body to the effect that he is able and willing to act as a foundation governor; or

           (c)   the date when a person other than the original governor takes office in the post by virtue of which the *ex officio* governorship exists.

      (7)   This Regulation and paragraphs 4 and 5 of Schedule 7 shall not prevent a governor:

           (a)   from being elected or appointed for a further term; or

           (b)   from being disqualified, by virtue of provision made under these Regulations, for continuing to hold office.

Resignation

17   (1)   Any governor of a school may at any time resign his office.

      (2)   An *ex officio* foundation governor may resign as governor by refusing to act as such a governor, either permanently or temporarily, but his resignation shall not prejudice the *ex officio* governorship of his successor in the post from which the *ex officio* governorship derives.

      (3)   A headteacher of a school may resign as governor by choosing at any time not to be a governor.

Removal

18   (1)   Subject to paragraph (2) and to Part VIII (transitional provisions), any governor of a school who was appointed otherwise than by being co-opted may be removed from office by the person or persons who appointed him.

      (2)   The power of removal in paragraph (1) does not apply in respect of any elected governor, parent governor who has been appointed rather than elected, or partnership governor.

(3) (a) The governing body may, in accordance with the procedure set out in Regulation 19, remove any additional co-opted governor at the request of a nominating body, if the governing body thinks fit.

      (b) A nominating body proposing the removal of an additional co-opted governor shall inform the governor in question (in writing) of the reasons why they are proposing his removal.

      (c) In these Regulations a 'nominating body' means any person from whom nominations were sought for the purpose of appointing, and who nominated, the additional co-opted governor in question.

      (d) In sub-paragraph (a) 'request' means a written request, setting out the reasons for the proposed removal.

(4) Any co-opted governor (other than an additional co-opted governor), may be removed from office by the governing body in accordance with the procedure set out in Regulation 19.

Removal of governors by the governing body

19 (1) This regulation applies in relation to the removal of a governor from office in accordance with Regulation 18(3) or (4).

    (2) Subject to paragraphs (3) and (4), a resolution to remove a governor from office which is passed at a meeting of the governing body shall not have effect unless:

      (a) it is confirmed by a resolution passed at a second meeting of the governing body held not less than 14 days after the first meeting ('the second meeting'); and

      (b) the matter of the governor's removal from office is specified as an item of business on the agenda for each of those meetings.

    (3) In relation to the removal of an additional co-opted governor, before the governing body resolve at the second meeting whether to confirm the resolution to remove the governor from office, the clerk shall give the reasons for removal provided by the nominating body (although the nominating body may also make representations if they so wish) and the governor whom it is proposed to remove shall be given an opportunity to make a statement in response.

    (4) In relation to the removal of a co-opted governor (other than an additional co-opted governor), before the governing body resolve at the second meeting whether to confirm the resolution to remove the governor from office, the governor or governors proposing his removal shall at that meeting state their reasons for doing so and the governor whom it is proposed to remove shall be given an opportunity to make a statement in response.

Notice of resignation or removal

20 (1) Where a governor of a school resigns his office or is removed from office (other than by the governing body), the governor or, where he is removed from office, those removing him, shall give written notice thereof to the clerk to the governing body of the school.

    (2) At any time when a headteacher of a school chooses to be or not to be a governor thereof, he shall give written notice of that decision to the clerk to the governing body of the school.

PART IV

CLERKS

Application and interpretation

21 (1) Regulations 23 and 25 do not apply to the appointment of the first clerk to the temporary governing body of a new school.

    (2) Subject to paragraph (1), in Regulations 22 to 25 references to a community, voluntary controlled, community special, foundation, voluntary-aided or foundation special school, or to a maintained school, include a new school which will be such a school.

    (3) Any provision in this Part relating to the dismissal of a clerk to the governing body is without prejudice to any rights and liabilities which the clerk may have if he is employed under a contract of employment.

Clerk to the governing body: restrictions

22 (1) On and after 1 April 2000:

   (a)   the clerk to the governing body of a maintained school shall not be a member of the governing body;

   (b)   the headteacher of a maintained school shall not serve as clerk to the governing body.

   (2) Notwithstanding paragraph (1), the governing body may, where the clerk fails to attend a meeting of theirs, appoint any one of their number to act as clerk for the purposes of that meeting.

Appointment of the clerk to the governing body

23 (1) This Regulation is subject to Regulation 25.

   (2) Where there is a vacancy in the office of clerk to the governing body**(a)** of a community, voluntary-controlled or community special school, the local education authority shall appoint a person selected by the governing body to be the clerk.

   (3) Where there is a vacancy in the office of clerk to the governing body of a foundation, voluntary-aided or foundation special school, the governing body shall appoint a clerk.

Dismissal of the clerk

24 (1) This Regulation is subject to Regulation 25.

   (2) Where the governing body of a community, voluntary-controlled or community special school determine that the clerk to the governing body should be dismissed:

   (a)   they shall notify the authority in writing of their determination and the reasons for it; and

   (b)   the authority shall dismiss the clerk to the governing body on receipt of the notification from the governing body.

   (3) The governing body of a foundation, voluntary-aided or foundation special school may determine that the clerk should be dismissed.

Appointment and dismissal of the clerk where the school does not have a delegated budget

25 (1) If at any time a maintained school does not have a delegated budget the following provisions shall apply:

   (2) In the case of a community, voluntary-controlled or community special school, the local education authority may appoint and dismiss the clerk to the governing body as the authority think fit.

   (3) The authority shall in connection with the exercise of their functions under paragraph (2) consult the governing body to such extent as the authority think fit.

   (4) In the case of a foundation, voluntary-aided or foundation special school:

   (a)   except with the consent of the local education authority, the governing body shall not:

      (i)   appoint a clerk, or

      (ii)   dismiss the clerk;

   (b)   the local education authority may give the governing body directions requiring them to dismiss the clerk.

First clerk to the temporary governing body

26 (1) The first clerk to the temporary governing body of a new school which will be a community, voluntary-controlled, or community special school, or a foundation or foundation special school, proposals for the establishment of which were published by the local education authority, shall be appointed by the local education authority.

   (2) The first clerk to the temporary governing body of a new school not referred to in paragraph (1) which will be a foundation or voluntary-aided school shall be appointed by the promoters of the school.

(a)   Part VIII of these Regulations contains provisions relating to clerks to governing bodies and temporary governing bodies on transition to the new schools framework under the 1998 Act.

Clerking on transition to the permanent governing body

27   The person who was the clerk to the temporary governing body of a new school shall act as clerk to the governing body who succeed them, pending the appointment of their clerk.

PART V

MEETINGS AND PROCEEDINGS OF GOVERNING BODIES

Interpretation

28   In this Part, except where the context otherwise requires, any reference to a school is a reference to a maintained school or a new school.

Chairman and vice-chairman of the governing body

29   (1)   The governing body of a school (other than the temporary governing body of a new school) shall each school year, at their first meeting in that year, elect a chairman and a vice-chairman from among their number (subject however to paragraph (2)).

(2)   A governor who is employed to work, or is a registered pupil, at the school in question shall not be eligible for election as chairman or vice-chairman.

(3)   Subject to paragraphs (4) and (5), the chairman or vice-chairman shall hold office as such until his successor has been elected in accordance with paragraph (1).

(4)   The chairman or vice-chairman may at any time resign his office by giving notice in writing to the clerk to the governing body.

(5)   The chairman or vice-chairman shall cease to hold office if:

(a)   he ceases to be a member of the governing body;

(b)   he is employed to work at the school in question;

(c)   in the case of the chairman, he is removed from office in accordance with Regulation 30; or

(d)   in the case of the vice-chairman, he is elected in accordance with paragraph (6) to fill a vacancy in the office of chairman.

(6)   Where by reason of any of the matters referred to in paragraphs (4) or (5) a vacancy arises in the office of chairman or vice-chairman, the governing body shall at their next meeting elect one of their number to fill that vacancy (subject however to paragraph (2)).

(7)   Subject to paragraphs (8) and (9), where the chairman is absent from any meeting or there is at the time a vacancy in the office of the chairman, the vice-chairman shall act as the chairman for the purposes of the meeting.

(8)   Where in the circumstances referred to in paragraph (7) the vice-chairman is absent from the meeting or there is at the time a vacancy in the office of vice-chairman, the governing body shall elect one of their number to act as a chairman for the purposes of that meeting, provided that the governor elected shall not be a person who is employed to work at the school, or a registered pupil thereat.

(9)   The clerk to the governing body shall act as chairman during that part of any meeting at which the chairman is elected, but for these purposes Regulation 38(2) (chairman's casting vote) shall not apply.

(10)   Any election of the chairman or vice-chairman which is contested shall be held by secret ballot.

(11)   (a)   The following provisions of this paragraph shall apply on and after 1 April 2000.

(b)   Before any meeting at which the chairman is to be elected, the clerk to the governing body shall invite members of the governing body of the school to inform him whether they are willing to stand for election as chairman.

(c)   The agenda for the meeting at which the chairman is to be elected shall list the names of persons who have informed the clerk that they are willing to stand for election.

(d)   If no person is listed on the agenda referred to in sub-paragraph (c) as willing to stand for election as chairman, members of the governing body may state at the meeting at which the chairman is to be elected whether or not they are willing to stand for election.

(e)   Sub-paragraphs (b) to (d) apply in relation to the election of the vice-chairman as they apply in relation to the election of the chairman.

Removal from office of the chairman of the governing body

30 (1) Subject to the following provisions of this Regulation, the governing body (other than the temporary governing body of a new school) may remove the chairman from office.

(2) Subject to paragraphs (3) and (4), a resolution to remove the chairman from office which is passed at a meeting of the governing body shall not have effect unless:

(a) it is confirmed by a resolution passed at a second meeting of the governing body held not less than 14 days after the first meeting ('the second meeting'); and

(b) the matter of the chairman's removal from office is specified as an item of business on the agenda for each of those meetings.

(3) Where the governing body include additional governors or additional foundation governors appointed under Section 27 of the School Inspections Act 1996**(a)** or Section 16 or 18 of the 1998 Act, paragraph (4) shall apply instead of paragraph (2).

(4) A resolution to remove the chairman from office which is passed at a meeting of the governing body shall not have effect unless the matter of the chairman's removal from office is specified as an item of business on the agenda for that meeting.

(5) Before the governing body resolve at the relevant meeting on whether to confirm the resolution to remove the chairman from office, the governor or governors proposing his removal shall at that meeting state their reasons for doing so and the chairman shall be given an opportunity to make a statement in response.

(6) In paragraph (5), the reference to the relevant meeting is:

(a) in any case to which paragraph (2) applies, to the second meeting held to consider the chairman's removal; and

(b) in any case to which paragraph (4) applies, to any meeting held to consider the chairman's removal from office.

Chairman and vice-chairman of temporary governing bodies

31 (1) The temporary governing body of a new school shall, at their first meeting, elect a chairman and vice-chairman from among their number (subject however to paragraph (9))**(b)**.

(2) The chairman or vice-chairman of a temporary governing body may at any time resign his office by giving notice in writing to the clerk to the temporary governing body.

(3) The chairman or vice-chairman of a temporary governing body shall cease to hold office as such if:

(a) he ceases to be a member of the temporary governing body;

(b) he is employed to work at the new school; or

(c) in the case of a vice-chairman, he is elected in pursuance of paragraph (4) to fill a vacancy in the office of chairman.

(4) Where by reason of any of the matters referred to in paragraphs (2) or (3) a vacancy arises in the office of chairman or vice-chairman, the temporary governing body shall at their next meeting elect one of their number to fill that vacancy (subject however to paragraph (9)).

(5) Subject to paragraphs (6) and (7), where the chairman is absent from any meeting or there is at the time a vacancy in the office of the chairman, the vice-chairman shall act as the chairman of the purposes of the meeting.

(6) Where in the circumstances referred to in paragraph (5) the vice-chairman is absent from the meeting or there is at the time a vacancy in the office of vice-chairman, the temporary governing body shall elect one of their number to act as a chairman for the purposes of that meeting, but subject to paragraph (9).

(7) The clerk to the temporary governing body shall act as chairman during that part of any meeting at which the chairman is elected, but for these purposes Regulation 38(2) (chairman's casting vote) shall not apply.

(a) 1996 c 57. Such governors continue in office from 1 September by virtue of Regulation 57 of the Second Transitional Regulations.

(b) Part VIII makes provision in relation to chairmen and vice-chairmen of temporary governing bodies of new schools on transition to the new schools framework under the 1998 Act.

(8)   Any election of the chairman or vice-chairman which is contested shall be held by secret ballot.

(9)   A member of the temporary governing body of a new school who is:

    (a)   the headteacher of the new school; or

    (b)   a person employed to work at the new school or, in the opinion of the other temporary governors, likely to become so employed,

shall not be eligible for election as chairman or vice-chairman of the temporary governing body of the new school or as a chairman of a meeting thereof but, subject as aforesaid, every temporary governor shall be so eligible.

Right of the headteacher to attend meetings

32   (1)   A headteacher of a school who is not a governor thereof shall be entitled to attend any meeting of the governing body of the school subject, however, to Part VII.

    (2)   Where two or more schools are to be discontinued ('the discontinued schools'), and the registered pupils at those schools, or a substantial number of those pupils, are expected to transfer to a new school, the headteachers of the discontinued schools shall be entitled to attend any meeting of the temporary governing body of the new school until a headteacher is appointed for that new school, subject, however, to Part VII.

Public access to meetings

33   Any question whether any person who is not:

    (1)   a member of the governing body;

    (2)   the clerk to the governing body; or

    (3)   a headteacher entitled under Regulation 32 to attend meetings of the governing body of a school,

should be allowed to attend meetings thereof shall be determined by the governing body.

Convening of meetings of the governing body

34   (1)   The governing body of every school, other than a new school, shall hold at least one meeting in every school term.

    (2)   The temporary governing body of a new school shall hold a meeting as often as occasion may require.

    (3)   Meetings of the governing body shall be convened by the clerk to the governing body; and, without prejudice to paragraph (5), in exercising his functions under this paragraph the clerk to the governing body shall comply with any direction:

        (a)   given by the governing body; or

        (b)   given by the chairman of the governing body or, in his absence or where there is a vacancy in the office of chairman, the vice-chairman of the governing body, so far as such direction is not inconsistent with any direction given as mentioned in sub-paragraph (a).

    (4)   Any three members of the governing body may, by notice in writing given to the clerk to the governing body, requisition a meeting thereof; and it shall be the duty of the clerk, subject to paragraph (5), to convene such a meeting as soon as is reasonably practicable.

    (5)   Each member of the governing body of a school, the headteacher (if he is not a member of the governing body) and the local education authority by whom the school is maintained, shall be given at least seven clear days before the date of a meeting:

        (a)   notice in writing thereof, signed by the clerk to the governing body; and

        (b)   a copy of the agenda for the meeting:

provided that where the chairman or, in his absence or where there is a vacancy in the office of chairman, the vice-chairman, so determines on the ground that there are matters demanding urgent consideration, it shall be sufficient if the written notice of a meeting, and the copy of the agenda therefor, are given within such shorter period as he directs.

    (6)   The power of the chairman or vice-chairman under paragraph (5) to direct that a meeting be held within a shorter period shall not apply in relation to any meeting at which the chairman's removal from office is to be considered in accordance with Regulation 30 or a co-opted governor's removal is to be considered in accordance with Regulation 19.

(7)   For the purposes of paragraph (5):

    (a)   notice of a meeting, and a copy of the agenda therefor, may be given to a person by leaving it at, or sending it by post to, his usual place of residence;

    (b)   'headteacher' means any headteacher entitled, by virtue of Regulation 32, to attend the meetings of the governing body.

(8)   The convening of a meeting and the proceedings conducted thereat shall not be invalidated by reason of any individual not having received written notice of the meeting or a copy of the agenda therefor.

Rescission and variation of resolutions

35   A resolution to rescind or vary a resolution carried at a previous meeting of the governing body shall not be proposed at a meeting of the governing body unless the consideration of the rescission or variation of the previous resolution is a specific item of business on the agenda for that meeting.

Termination and adjournment of meetings

36   (1)   If the number of members of the governing body who are present at the time and place appointed for a meeting thereof does not constitute a quorum for the purposes of Regulation 37 the meeting shall not be held.

    (2)   A meeting of the governing body shall be terminated forthwith if:

    (a)   the governing body so resolve; or

    (b)   the number of members present ceases to constitute a quorum for a meeting of the governing body in accordance with Regulation 37.

    (3)   Where in accordance with paragraph (1) or (2) a meeting is not held or is terminated before all the matters specified as items of business on the agenda for the meeting have been disposed of, a further meeting shall be convened by the clerk to the governing body as soon as is reasonably practicable.

    (4)   Where the governing body resolve in accordance with paragraph (2)(a) to adjourn a meeting before all the items of business on the agenda have been disposed of, the governing body shall before doing so determine the time and date at which a further meeting is to be held for the purposes of completing the consideration of those items, and they shall direct the clerk to the governing body to convene a meeting accordingly.

    (5)   In any case falling within paragraph (4) above, the governing body may determine that the further meeting referred to in that paragraph shall be held at a date and time which, because of its proximity in time to the adjourned meeting, would not allow the clerk to the governing body a sufficient period for the purpose of giving the notice required by Regulation 34:

    provided that in such a case the clerk to the governing body shall use his best endeavours to secure that any member of the governing body not present at the first meeting is informed of the time and date of the further meeting.

Quorum

37   (1)   The quorum for a meeting of the governing body, and any vote on any matter thereat, shall, subject to paragraph (2), be any three members of that body, or, where greater, any one-third (rounded up to a whole number) of the membership when complete.

    (2)   Subject to paragraph (3), the quorum for the purposes of:

    (a)   appointing a parent governor or partnership governor;

    (b)   co-opting governors (otherwise than as foundation governors);

    (c)   co-opting temporary governors(a);

    (d)   appointing members of, or determining any question relating to, any committee established under these Regulations or any headteacher or deputy headteacher selection panel under Schedule 16 or 17 to the 1998 Act;

(a)   Regulations under Section 44 of the 1998 Act will make provision for the constitution of temporary governing bodies.

(e)   any vote on the removal of a member of the governing body in accordance with Regulation 19;

(f)   any vote on the removal of the chairman of the governing body in accordance with Regulation 30; or

(g)   making arrangements for an Education Action Forum to discharge any function on behalf of the governing body or assume full responsibility for the discharge of any function of the governing body,

shall be any two-thirds (rounded up to a whole number) of the persons who are at the time members of the governing body entitled to vote on those respective matters.

(3)   In any case to which paragraphs (3) and (4) of Regulation 30 apply, paragraph (2) shall have effect as if, for the purposes set out in paragraph (2)(f), the reference to two-thirds were a reference to one-half.

Proceedings of the governing body

38   (1)   Subject to paragraph (2), every question to be decided at a meeting of the governing body shall be determined by a majority of the votes of the members present and voting on the question.

(2)   Subject to Regulations 29(9) and 31(7), where there is an equal division of votes the chairman or, as the case may be, the person who is acting as chairman for the purposes of the meeting, shall have a second or casting vote.

(3)   The proceedings of the governing body of a school shall not be invalidated by:

(a)   any vacancy among their number;

(b)   any defect in the election, appointment or nomination of any governor, or the continuation in office of any governor by virtue of the First Transitional Regulations or the Second Transitional Regulations; or

(c)   the school having more governors of a particular category than are provided for by the instrument of government, pending removal of the surplus governors pursuant to paragraph 17 of Schedule 9 to the 1998 Act.

Minutes of meetings

39   (1)   The minutes of the proceedings of a meeting of the governing body shall, subject to paragraph (2), be drawn up and entered into a book kept for the purpose by the person acting as clerk to the governing body for the purposes of the meeting; and shall be signed (subject to the approval of the governing body) at the same or next subsequent meeting by the person acting as chairman thereof.

(2)   The minutes of proceedings of meetings may be entered on loose-leaf pages consecutively numbered; but in that case the person signing the minutes shall initial each page.

(3)   The person acting as clerk to the governing body for the purposes of any meeting shall record immediately before the entry recording the minutes of that meeting in the book or pages used for that purpose the names of those members of the governing body and of any other person present at the meeting concerned.

(4)   On request made in that behalf by the local education authority by whom a school is maintained, in relation to a particular meeting or generally, that authority shall be supplied with a copy of the draft or signed minutes of the relevant meeting or (as the case may be) of any meeting of the governing body of the school.

Publication of minutes and papers

40   (1)   Subject to paragraph (2), the governing body shall ensure that a copy of:

(a)   the agenda for every meeting of the governing body;

(b)   the draft minutes of every such meeting, if they have been approved by the person acting as chairman of that meeting;

(c)   the signed minutes of every such meeting; and

(d)   any report, document or other paper considered at any such meeting,

are, as soon as is reasonably practicable, made available at the school to persons wishing to inspect them.

(2) There may be excluded from any item required to be made available in pursuance of paragraph (1), any material relating to:

(a) a named teacher or other person employed, or proposed to be employed, at the school;

(b) a named pupil at, or candidate for admission to, the school; and

(c) any matter which, by reason of its nature, the governing body are satisfied should remain confidential.

(3) This regulation does not apply in relation to temporary governing bodies of new schools.

Delegation of functions

41 (1) Subject to any other statutory provision concerning the exercise of functions on behalf of the governing body and to Regulation 42, the governing body of a school may, in such circumstances as they think fit, delegate any of the functions conferred on them by or under any enactment to any committee established by them or to any member of the governing body or to the headteacher.

(2) Where the governing body have delegated functions to an individual or committee under paragraph (1) or to a committee under Regulation 42(4) or (5), this shall not prevent the governing body from exercising those functions themselves.

Restrictions on delegation

42 (1) The governing body may not delegate under Regulation 41 (1) functions referred to in paragraphs (2) to (5) of this Regulation or functions relating to the powers conferred and the duties imposed on governing bodies by or under:

(a) Section 394 of the 1996 Act (which relates to applications to advisory councils concerning the requirements for Christian collective worship);

(b) Section 403 of the 1996 Act (which relates to sex education);

(c) Section 406 or 407 of the 1996 Act (which relate to the prohibition of political indoctrination and the balanced treatment of political issues respectively);

(d) Section 457 of the 1996 Act (which relates to policies on charges and remissions);

(e) Section 12(2) of the 1998 Act (which relates to the making of arrangements for the discharge of governing body functions by or ceding of governing body functions to an Education Action Forum and the request to an Education Action Forum to cease discharging functions on their behalf);

(f) Sections 28, 29, 30 or 31 of, or paragraph 5(4) of Schedule 6 to, the 1998 Act (which relate to alteration or discontinuance of maintained schools);

(g) Sections 28 or 31 of the 1998 Act as they have effect (by virtue of Regulations under Schedule 8 to the 1998 Act) in relation to proposals made under that Schedule (which relates to change of category of maintained schools);

(h) Section 41 of the 1998 Act (which relates to the times of school sessions and the dates of school terms and holidays);

(i) Section 42 of the 1998 Act (which relates to the governors' annual report to parents) in so far as approval of the governors' report is concerned;

(j) the local education authority's scheme under Section 48(1) of the 1998 Act, to the extent that it requires the governing body to give their approval to the first formal budget plan of the financial year;

(k) Section 61 (1) to (3) of the 1998 Act (which relate to school discipline policies);

(l) Sections 88, 89, 90(8) or 91 of the 1998 Act (which relate to the determination of admission arrangements), Section 90(1) of the 1998 Act (which relates to the decision to object to the admissions arrangements of another admissions authority), Section 93 of or Schedule 23 to the 1998 Act (which relate to fixing admission numbers and variation of standard numbers), or Section 94 of the 1998 Act (in so far as it relates to the determination of appeal arrangements by the governing body);

(m) Section 110(1) or (7) of the 1998 Act (which relate to adoption and review of home-school agreements);

(n) paragraphs 4(4) or (5) of Schedule 11 to the 1998 Act (which relate to the regulation of procedure);

    (o)   paragraph 6 of Schedule 16 or paragraphs 7 or 30 of Schedule 17 to the 1998 Act (which relate to headteacher and deputy headteacher selection panels);

    (p)   paragraphs 10 to 16 of Schedule 16 or paragraphs 11 to 16 of Schedule 17 to the 1998 Act (which relate to appointment of teachers other than the headteacher or deputy headteacher**(a)**);

    (q)   paragraph 27(2) of Schedule 16 or paragraph 24(2) of Schedule 17 to the 1998 Act (which relate to the making of arrangements for appeals in cases of dismissal);

    (r)   paragraph 2 of Schedule 20 to the 1998 Act (which relates to arrangements for collective worship);

    (s)   Regulations 29 or 31 (which relate to the appointment of the chairman and vice-chairman of a governing body or temporary governing body);

    (t)   Regulation 30 (which relates to removal of the chairman of the governing body);

    (u)   Regulation 34(1) or (2) (which relate to the requirement to hold a governing body meeting once a term, or a meeting of the temporary governing body as often as occasion may require);

    (v)   statutory provisions relating to the decision to delegate functions, or the establishment, constitution, proceedings and review of committees, including selection panels;

    (w)   statutory provisions relating to the contents, preparation or variation of the instrument of government;

    (x)   statutory provisions relating to the appointment, co-option or removal of governors including temporary governors; or

    (y)   Part IV of the Education (School Information) (England) Regulations 1998**(b)** (which relates to information to be published by governing bodies) in so far as approval of the school prospectus (referred to in Regulation 11 of those Regulations) is concerned.

(2)   (a)   The following functions of the governing body of a school shall be delegated to a committee, to be known as the staff dismissal committee, in accordance with Regulation 47:

        (i)   at a community, voluntary-controlled or community special school, the initial determination under paragraph 25 of Schedule 16 to the 1998 Act that any person employed by the local education authority to work at the school should cease to work there;

        (ii)   at a foundation, voluntary-aided or foundation special school, the initial decision that a person employed to work at the school should have his contract of employment with the governing body terminated or should not have that contract renewed (except where the dismissal is pursuant to a direction of the local education authority under Section 55(5) of the 1998 Act);

        (iii)   the hearing of representations in relation to a decision which must be delegated under this sub-paragraph.

    (b)   The hearing of any appeal in respect of a decision which must be delegated under sub-paragraph (a) shall be delegated to a committee, known as the dismissal appeal committee, in accordance with Regulation 47.

(3)   The governing body of a school shall in accordance with Regulation 48 establish a committee, to be known as the pupil discipline committee, to discharge the functions conferred on them by Sections 65 to 68 of the 1998 Act (which relate to exclusion of pupils).

(4)   Any power of the governing body of a school to determine whether any child should be admitted to the school shall not be delegated to an individual, but may be delegated to a committee, to be known as an admissions committee, in accordance with Regulation 49.

(a)   These functions are not delegated under Regulation 41 because there are specified powers of delegation (to one or more governors, the headteacher, or one or more governors and the headteacher) in paragraph 17 of Schedule 16 and paragraph 17 of Schedule 17 to the 1998 Act.

(b)   SI 1998/2526, amended by SI 1999/251.

(5)   The functions of the governing body of a school:

     (a)   under Section 63 of the 1998 Act (which relates to school attendance targets);

     (b)   under Section 439(7) of the 1996 Act (which relates to school attendance orders);

     (c)   under Section 95(2) or 97(3) of the 1998 Act (which relate to appeals against decisions of the local education authority to admit a child and referral to the Secretary of State in respect of a direction made by the local education authority to admit a child respectively);

     (d)   which consist of the taking of any decision as to the particulars of premises to be submitted to the Secretary of State for approval under Section 544 of the 1996 Act; or

     (e)   relating to the appointment or dismissal of the clerk to the governing body under Part IV,

shall not be delegated to an individual but may be delegated to a committee.

Delegation of functions to the chairman and vice-chairman in cases of urgency

43   (1)   The chairman of the governing body of a school shall have power, where in his opinion the circumstances mentioned in paragraph (2) apply, to exercise any function of the governing body which can be delegated under Regulation 41 (1).

     (2)   The circumstances are that a delay in exercising the function would be likely to be seriously detrimental to the interests of the school, or to the interests of any registered pupil at the school, or his parent, or a person employed to work at the school.

     (3)   In paragraph (2), 'a delay' means a delay for a period extending beyond the day preceding the earliest date on which it would be reasonably practicable for a meeting of the governing body, or a committee of the governing body to whom the function in question has been delegated, to be held.

     (4)   Where it appears to the vice-chairman:

       (a)   that the circumstances mentioned in paragraph (2) apply, and

       (b)   that the chairman (whether by reason of a vacancy in his office or otherwise) would be unable to exercise the function in question before the detriment referred to in that sub-paragraph is suffered,

the reference in paragraph (1) to the chairman shall have effect as if it were a reference to the vice-chairman.

Reporting to the governing body following the exercise of delegated functions

44   (1)   This regulation applies where any function of the governing body of a school has been delegated to or is otherwise exercisable by a member of the governing body (including the chairman or vice-chairman), the headteacher, or a committee established by them.

     (2)   Any member, headteacher or committee to whom a function of the governing body has been delegated or who has otherwise exercised a function of the governing body shall report to the governing body in respect of any action taken or decision made with respect to the exercise of that function at the meeting of the governing body immediately following the taking of the action or the making of the decision.

PART VI

COMMITTEES OF GOVERNING BODIES

Interpretation and application

45   (1)   In this Part, except where the context otherwise requires, any reference to a school is a reference to a maintained school or a new school.

     (2)   This Part shall not apply in relation to headteacher and deputy headteacher selection panels.

Establishment and constitution of committees of the governing body

46   (1)   Subject to paragraphs (2) to (4) of Regulation 42, the governing body of a school may establish such committees as they think fit for the purpose of exercising on their behalf such functions as they may delegate to a committee in accordance with Regulation 41 or 42.

(2) Subject to Regulations 47, 48 and 49, and to paragraph 17 of Schedule 16 and paragraph 17 of Schedule 17 to the 1998 Act:

(a) the constitution, membership and proceedings of any committee of the governing body shall be determined by the governing body;

(b) the establishment, terms of reference, constitution and membership of any committee of the governing body shall be reviewed at least once in every 12 months;

(c) the membership of any committee of the governing body may include persons who are not members of the governing body, provided that a majority of members of any such committee shall be members of the governing body;

(d) subject to sub-paragraph (e), the members of the committee who are not members of the governing body shall not be entitled to vote in any proceedings of the committee;

(e) the governing body may determine that some or all of the members of a committee who are not members of the governing body shall be entitled to vote in any proceedings of the committee;

(f) no vote on any matter shall be taken at a meeting of a committee of the governing body unless the majority of members of the committee present are members of the governing body of the school;

(g) the chair at any meeting of a committee of the governing body shall be taken by the chairman thereof, except that when he is absent those present shall elect from among their number a person to take the chair at the meeting during such absence;

(h) no person who is:

(i) employed to work at the school;

(ii) a registered pupil thereat; or

(iii) not a member of the governing body,

shall act as chairman of a committee of the governing body.

Staff dismissal committee and dismissal appeal committee

47 (1) Subject to paragraph (6), the staff dismissal committee referred to in Regulation 42(2)(a) shall include not less than three members of the governing body.

(2) The dismissal appeal committee referred to in Regulation 42(2)(b) shall include no fewer members of the governing body than the staff dismissal committee, the decision of which is subject to appeal.

(3) Where a dismissal appeal committee is considering an appeal against a decision of the staff dismissal committee, no member of the staff dismissal committee whose decision is subject to appeal shall take part in the proceedings of the dismissal appeal committee.

(4) The headteacher of the school shall not be a member of the staff dismissal committee or the dismissal appeal committee.

(5) No member of the staff dismissal committee or the dismissal appeal committee who is not a member of the governing body shall be entitled to vote in any proceedings of the committee in question.

(6) Where it is not reasonably practicable for the staff dismissal committee and the dismissal appeal committee each to include three members of the governing body, the staff dismissal committee shall include two members of the governing body.

Pupil discipline committee

48 (1) The pupil discipline committee referred to in Regulation 42(3) shall consist of either three or five members of the governing body, but shall not include the headteacher.

(2) The quorum for a meeting of the pupil discipline committee and any vote on any matter thereat shall be three members of the committee.

(3) Despite Regulation 42(3), the chairman of the pupil discipline committee may exercise any function conferred on the governing body by subsections (2) to (4) of Section 66 of the 1998 Act in a case where:

(a)   a pupil has been excluded for a fixed period in circumstances in which he would, as a result of the exclusion, lose an opportunity to take any public examination; and

(b)   it appears to the chairman that it would not be practical for a quorate meeting of the committee to take place for any purpose referred to in those subsections before the time when the pupil would be due to take that examination.

Admissions committee

49   (1)   Where the governing body establish an admissions committee referred to in Regulation 42(4) that committee shall consist of:

(a)   the headteacher of the school (who shall be entitled to vote whether or not he is a governor); and

(b)   at least two other persons who are members of the governing body.

(2)   In the case of any school which has more than one headteacher, the reference in paragraph (1)(a) to the headteacher shall be interpreted as a reference to one of the headteachers.

Disqualification of members of governing body committees

50   (1)   No person shall be qualified for membership of a committee of the governing body of a school unless he is aged 18 or over at the date of his appointment.

(2)   Subject to paragraph (4) the following paragraphs of Schedule 5 shall apply for the purpose of setting out the circumstances in which a person who is not a governor of a school is disqualified for holding or continuing in office as a member of a committee of the governing body of that school:

(a)   paragraph 2 (mental disorder);

(b)   paragraph 5 (bankruptcy);

(c)   paragraph 6 (disqualification of company directors);

(d)   paragraph 7 (disqualification of charity trustees);

(e)   paragraph 8 (persons whose employment is prohibited or restricted);

(f)   paragraph 9 (persons disqualified for being proprietors of independent schools);

(g)   paragraph 10 (criminal convictions).

(3)   Where, by virtue of paragraph (2):

(a)   a person becomes disqualified for holding, or for continuing to hold, office as a member of a committee of the governing body of a school; and

(b)   he is, or is proposed to become, such a member,

he shall upon becoming so disqualified give written notice of that fact to the clerk to the governing body.

(4)   For the purposes of paragraph (2):

(a)   in the provisions referred to in paragraph (2)(a) to (g), for references to 'governor' there shall be substituted 'member of a committee of the governing body'; and

(b)   in paragraph 10 of Schedule 5:

(i)   sub-paragraph (2) shall be omitted; and

(ii)   there shall be omitted (in each place in which they appear) the words 'or election', 'or, as the case may be, on which he would otherwise have become a governor *ex officio*' and 'or as the case may be, since he became a governor *ex officio*.'

Clerks to committees

51   (1)   (a)   In establishing any committee referred to in Regulations 47, 48 or 49, the governing body shall appoint a clerk to the committee.

(b)   In establishing any other committee, the governing body may appoint a clerk to the committee.

(2)   The governing body of a school may dismiss any clerk appointed by them under paragraph (1).

(3)   On and after 1 April 2000:

(a)   the clerk to any committee referred to in Regulations 47, 48 or 49 shall not be a member of the governing body or a member of the committee concerned;

(b)   the headteacher shall not serve as clerk to any committee referred to in Regulations 47, 48 or 49.

(4)   Notwithstanding paragraph (1), a committee of the governing body may, where their clerk fails to attend a meeting of theirs, appoint any one of their number to act as clerk for the purposes of that meeting.

Meetings of committees

52   (1)   Each member of a committee of the governing body of a school, and the headteacher of the school, shall be given, at least seven clear days before the date of a meeting:

(a)   notice in writing thereof; and

(b)   a copy of the agenda for the meeting:

provided that where the chairman of the committee so determines on the ground that there are matters demanding urgent consideration, it shall be sufficient if the written notice of a meeting, and the copy of the agenda therefor, are given within such shorter periods as he directs.

(2)   For the purposes of paragraph (1) notice of a meeting, and a copy of the agenda therefor, may be given to a person by leaving it at, or sending it by post to, his usual place of residence.

Proceedings of committees

53   (1)   Subject to paragraph (4), every question to be decided at a meeting of a committee of the governing body shall be determined by a majority of the votes of the eligible members present and voting on the question, except that where there is an equal division of votes the person who is acting as chairman for the purposes of the meeting shall have a second or casting vote.

(2)   For the purposes of paragraph (1) an 'eligible member' means any person entitled to vote in the proceedings of the committee.

(3)   The proceedings of a committee of the governing body shall not be invalidated by:

(a)   any vacancy among their number; or

(b)   any defect in the appointment of any member of the committee.

(4)   Paragraphs (1) and (3) are subject to Regulation 46(2)(f).

Minutes of meetings of committees

54   (1)   The minutes of the proceedings of a meeting of a committee of the governing body shall, subject to paragraph (2), be drawn up and entered into a book kept for the purpose by the person acting as clerk to the committee for the purposes of the meeting; and shall be signed (subject to the approval of the committee) at the same or next subsequent meeting by the person acting as chairman thereof.

(2)   The minutes of proceedings of meetings may be entered on loose-leaf pages consecutively numbered; but in that case the person signing the minutes shall initial each page.

(3)   The person acting as clerk to a committee of the governing body for the purposes of any meeting shall record immediately before the entry recording the minutes of that meeting in the book or pages used for that purpose the names of those members of the committee and of any other person present at the meeting concerned.

(4)   On request made in that behalf by the local education authority by whom a school is maintained, in relation to a particular meeting or generally, that authority shall be supplied with a copy of the draft or signed minutes of the relevant meeting or (as the case may be) of any meeting of a committee of the governing body of the school.

Publication of minutes and papers of committees

55   (1)   Subject to paragraph (2), a committee of the governing body shall ensure that a copy of:

(a)   the agenda for every meeting of the committee;

(b)   the draft minutes of every such meeting, if they have been approved by the person acting as chairman of that meeting;

(c)   the signed minutes of every such meeting; and

(d)   any report, document or other paper considered at any such meeting, are, as soon as is reasonably practicable, made available at the school to persons wishing to inspect them.

(2) There may be excluded from any item required to be made available in pursuance of paragraph (1) any material relating to:

    (a) a named teacher or other person employed, or proposed to be employed, at the school;

    (b) a named pupil at, or candidate for admission to, the school; and

    (c) any matter which, by reason of its nature, the committee are satisfied should remain confidential.

(3) This regulation does not apply to a committee of a temporary governing body.

Access to committee meetings

56 (1) A headteacher of a school shall be entitled to attend any meeting of a committee of the governing body of the school, subject however to Part VII and to paragraph (2).

(2) Paragraph (1) shall not confer any additional right on the headteacher in relation to any committee referred to in Regulations 47,48 or 49, or in relation to any committee or selection panel exercising a function referred to in Schedule 16 or 17 to the 1998 Act.

(3) Where two or more schools are to be discontinued ('the discontinued schools') and the registered pupils at those schools, or a substantial number of those pupils, are expected to transfer to a new school, the headteachers of the discontinued schools shall be entitled to attend any meeting of a committee of the temporary governing body of the new school until a headteacher is appointed for that new school, subject, however, to Part VII.

(4) Any question whether any person who is not:

    (a) a member of a committee of the governing body;

    (b) the clerk to the committee; or

    (c) a headteacher entitled to attend meetings of the committee,

should be allowed to attend any meetings thereof shall be determined by the committee concerned.

PART VII

RESTRICTIONS ON PERSONS TAKING PART IN PROCEEDINGS

57 (1) In this Regulation and in Schedule 6:

    (a) any reference to a school is a reference to a maintained school or a new school;

    (b) 'relevant person' means a member of the governing body, a member of a committee of the governing body, the headteacher or any person acting as clerk to the governing body or committee;

    (c) any reference, however expressed, to a committee of the governing body includes, where applicable, a selection panel.

(2) Subject to any exception in these Regulations and to any other statutory provision:

    (a) where in relation to any matter there may be a conflict between the interests of a relevant person and the interests of the governing body; or

    (b) where a fair hearing is required and there is any reasonable doubt about a relevant person's ability to act impartially in relation to any matter,

that person, if present at a meeting of the governing body or a committee of the governing body at which the matter is the subject of consideration, shall withdraw from the meeting and not vote on the matter in question.

(3) Nothing in this Regulation or in Schedule 6 shall be construed as precluding the governing body, or a committee of the governing body:

    (a) from allowing a person who appears to them to be able to give evidence to attend any hearing conducted by them into any matter and to present his evidence; or

    (b) from hearing representations from a relevant person acting in a capacity other than that of a relevant person.

(4) Any person who is acting as the clerk to the governing body or a committee of the governing body shall not be required to withdraw from a meeting by this Regulation or

Schedule 6 unless his pay or disciplinary action against him is the subject of consideration, but if this Regulation or Schedule 6 would have otherwise required him to withdraw, he shall not act in any capacity other than that of clerk.

(5) A governor or member of a committee of the governing body shall not be prevented from considering or voting upon any matter by reason that he is a governor or a member of a committee of the governing body at more than one school and that the interests of any school at which he is a governor or a member of a committee conflict with the interests of any other school at which he is a governor or a member of a committee.

(6) Where there is any dispute as to whether a relevant person is required by this regulation or by Schedule 6 to withdraw from a meeting and not vote, that question shall be determined by the other members of the governing body or, as the case may be, the other members of the committee present at the meeting.

(7) Schedule 6 makes provision in connection with specified conflicts of interest and cases where a relevant person is required to withdraw from a meeting and not vote.

PART VIII

TRANSITIONAL PROVISIONS

58 (1) Schedule 7 makes provision in relation to:

(a) qualifications and disqualifications for office, terms of office and removal of governors; and

(b) clerks to, and chairmen and vice-chairmen of, governing bodies,

of maintained schools and new schools on transition to the new framework under the 1998 Act.

(2) Schedule 7 amends the First Transitional Regulations and the Second Transitional Regulations in so far as they apply to England.

Estelle Morris
Minister of State
28 July 1999   Department for Education and Employment

SCHEDULE 1

Regulation 6

ADDITIONAL CO-OPTED GOVERNORS

1   In this Schedule, 'sponsor', in relation to a school, means a person who gives, or has given, substantial financial assistance (which for these purposes includes benefits in kind other than the provision of services) to the school other than pursuant to any statutory obligation.

2   Where the school has one or more sponsors, the governing body may determine that the instrument of government shall provide for the governing body of the school to include such number of additional co-opted governors, nominated in accordance with paragraph 3, as may be determined by the governing body, not exceeding two.

3   Nominations for such appointments shall be sought from the school's sponsor, or (as the case may be) from any one or more of the school's sponsors.

4   Where the school is a participating school in relation to an education action zone, the governing body may determine that the instrument of government shall provide for the governing body of the school to include one additional co-opted governor nominated by the Education Action Forum for the zone in relation to which the school is a participating school.

SCHEDULE 2

Regulation 9

PARENT GOVERNORS

1   In this Schedule 'appropriate authority' has the same meaning as in Schedule 4 (elections).

2   (1) This paragraph applies to any maintained school in relation to which this Schedule applies(a), other than a community or foundation special school established in a hospital.

(a)   See Regulation 4.

(2)   In the case of a school to which this paragraph applies, parent governors shall be appointed by the governing body if:

    (a)   at least 50 per cent of the registered pupils at the school are boarders; and

    (b)   it would, in the opinion of the appropriate authority, be impracticable for there to be an election of parent governors.

3   In the case of a school which is a community or foundation special school established in a hospital, parent governors shall be appointed by the governing body, where, in the opinion of the appropriate authority, it is likely to be impracticable for there to be an election of parent governors.

4   At any maintained school in relation to which this Schedule applies, the number of parent governors required shall be made up by parent governors appointed by the governing body if:

    (a)   one or more vacancies of parent governors are required to be filled by election; and

    (b)   the number of parents standing for election is less than the number of vacancies.

5   Except where paragraph 6 applies, in appointing a parent governor**(a)** under this Schedule the governing body shall appoint:

    (a)   a person who is the parent of a registered pupil at the school; or

    (b)   where it is not reasonably practicable to do so, a person who is the parent of a child of compulsory school age.

6   (1)   Where the school is a community or foundation special school not established in a hospital, in appointing a parent governor under paragraph 2(2) or 4, the governing body shall appoint:

    (a)   a person who is the parent of a registered pupil at the school;

    (b)   a person who is the parent of a child of compulsory school age with special educational needs;

    (c)   a person who is a parent of a person of any age with special educational needs; or

    (d)   a person who is the parent of a child of compulsory school age.

(2)   The governing body shall only appoint a person referred to in sub-paragraph (1)(b), (c) or (d) if it is not reasonably practicable to appoint a person referred to in the provision in that sub-paragraph which immediately precedes it.

SCHEDULE 3

Regulation 9

PARTNERSHIP GOVERNORS

1   Where a partnership governor is required, the governing body shall seek nominations from parents of registered pupils at the school, and from such other persons in the community served by the school as they consider appropriate.

2   No person shall nominate for appointment, or appoint, a person as a partnership governor**(b)** unless:

    (a)   in the case of a person nominating himself, he considers himself to be from the community served by the school and committed to the good government and success of the school; and

    (b)   in any other case, he is satisfied that the nominee or appointee appears to be from the community served by the school and committed to the good government and success of the school.

3   (1)   In the case of a school which is a foundation special school without a foundation, the governing body shall in appointing partnership governors secure that at least one partnership governor is a person with experience of education for children with special educational needs.

(2)   In seeking nominations for partnership governors for a school within sub-paragraph (1) the governing body shall take such steps as are reasonably practicable to secure that persons making nominations are aware of the requirement in that sub-paragraph.

(a)   See also paragraph 13 of Schedule 5 for disqualifications for being appointed as a parent governor.

(b)   See also paragraph 15 of Schedule 5 for disqualifications for being a partnership governor.

4   Where a partnership governor is required, the governing body shall take such steps as are reasonably practicable to secure that every person who is known to them to be a parent of a registered pupil at the school is:

      (a)   informed that he is entitled to nominate persons for appointment as partnership governors; and

      (b)   informed about the procedures to be followed in making nominations.

5   Subject to paragraph 7(2), no member of the governing body may nominate a person for appointment as a partnership governor.

6   The governing body shall make all necessary arrangements for, and determine all other matters relating to, the nomination of partnership governors.

7   (1)   The governing body shall appoint such number of partnership governors as are required by the instrument of government from among eligible nominees.

      (2)   If:

           (a)   the number of eligible nominees is less than the number of vacancies; or

           (b)   in the case of a foundation special school at which a partnership governor with experience of education for children with special educational needs is required, no eligible nominee has such experience,

        the number of partnership governors required shall be made up by persons selected by the governing body who are eligible and meet the requirements for appointment.

8   Where the governing body make an appointment under paragraph 7(2) having rejected any person nominated by a parent or the community served by the school, they shall explain the reason for that decision to the local education authority and the person rejected.

SCHEDULE 4

Regulation 12

ELECTIONS

1   Subject to paragraphs 2 and 3, in this paragraph 'appropriate authority' means:

      (a)   in relation to a community, community special or voluntary-controlled school, the local education authority; and

      (b)   in relation to a voluntary-aided, foundation or foundation special school, the governing body.

2   Where a local education authority is the appropriate authority in relation to a school, that authority may delegate to the headteacher of the school any of their functions under this Schedule except their functions under paragraph 4.

3   The local education authority shall be the appropriate authority in relation to a school within paragraph 1 (b) if the governing body and the local education authority so agree.

4   The appropriate authority shall determine:

      (a)   for the purposes of an election of parent governors, any question whether a person is a parent of a registered pupil at the school;

      (b)   for the purposes of an election of teacher governors, any question whether a person is a teacher at the school;

      (c)   for the purposes of an election of staff governors, any question whether a person is employed under a contract of employment or a contract for services to work at the school otherwise than as a teacher.

5   Subject to paragraphs 6 to 9, the appropriate authority shall make all necessary arrangements for, and determine all other matters relating to, an election of parent governors, teacher governors, or staff governors.

6   The power conferred by paragraph 5:

      (a)   includes power to make provision as to qualifying dates; but

      (b)   does not include power to impose any requirement as to the minimum number of votes required to be cast for a candidate to be elected.

7   Any election of parent governors, teacher governors or staff governors which is contested shall be held by secret ballot.

8   The arrangements made under paragraph 5 shall, in the case of any election of a parent governor, provide for every person who is entitled to vote in the election to have an opportunity to do so by post, or, if he prefers, by having his ballot paper returned to the school by a registered pupil at the school.

9   Where a vacancy for a parent governor is required to be filled by election, the appropriate authority shall take such steps as are reasonably practicable to secure that every person who is known to them to be a parent of a registered pupil at the school is:

(a)   informed of the vacancy and that it is required to be filled by election;

(b)   informed that he is entitled to stand as a candidate, and vote, at the election; and

(c)   given an opportunity to do so.

SCHEDULE 5

Regulations 15 and 50

QUALIFICATIONS AND DISQUALIFICATIONS

General

1   (1)   No person shall be qualified for membership of a governing body of a school unless he is aged 18 or over at the date of his election or appointment.

(2)   No person shall at any time hold more than one governorship of the same school.

(3)   Subject to paragraphs 12 and 15, the fact that a person is qualified to be elected or appointed as a governor of a particular category at a school does not disqualify him for election or appointment or for continuing as a governor of any other category at that school.

Mental disorder

2   A person shall be disqualified for holding or for continuing to hold office as a governor of a school at any time when he is liable to be detained under the Mental Health Act 1983(a).

Governor of more than two schools

3   (1)   A person shall be disqualified for holding office as a governor of a school if, were he to continue in office as such on transition to the new schools framework, or be appointed or elected to that office, he would, on the date on which he would have so continued in office or on which the appointment or election would have taken effect, be a member of the governing body of more than two schools.

(2)   For the purposes of sub-paragraph (1) no account shall be taken of *ex officio* governorships, temporary governorships, or additional governorships of governors appointed under Section 27 of the School Inspections Act 1996(b) or Sections 16 or 18 of the 1998 Act.

(3)   Sub-paragraph (4) applies to a person who continues in office on transition to the new schools framework as, or who becomes, an *ex officio* member of the governing body of a relevant school and is an *ex officio* member of the governing body of more than two relevant schools.

(4)   A person to whom this sub-paragraph applies shall be disqualified for continuing to hold office as an *ex officio* governor of any relevant school unless that school is for the time being a designated school.

(5)   For the purposes of sub-paragraph (4), a designated school is a school designated by the *ex officio* governor, in accordance with sub-paragraph (6), by notice in writing to the clerk to the governing body of the school and to the clerk to the governing body of any other relevant school whose instrument of government provides for him to be an *ex officio* member.

(6)   A person to whom sub-paragraph (4) applies may designate one or two maintained schools provided that the number of governing bodies of relevant schools of which he will be an *ex officio* member shall be no more than two.

(7)   For the purposes of this paragraph, a relevant school is a maintained school at which the governing body conducting the school are constituted or partly constituted under an instrument of government made under Schedule 12 to the 1998 Act.

(a)   1983 c 20.

(b)   1996 c 57. See Regulation 57 of the Second Transitional Regulations.

Failure to attend meetings

4 (1) This paragraph shall apply in the case of any governor of a school who is not an *ex officio* governor.

(2) Such a governor who, without the consent of the governing body concerned, has failed to attend the meetings thereof for a continuous period of six months beginning with the date of a meeting, shall, on the expiry of that period, be disqualified for continuing to hold office as a governor of that school.

(3) Where a governor has sent an apology to the clerk to the governing body before a meeting which he does not propose to attend, the minutes of the meeting shall record the governing body's consent or otherwise to his absence and a copy of the minutes shall be sent to the governor concerned at his normal place of residence.

(4) In relation to a governor who has continued in office on transition to the new schools framework, the period before 1 September 1999 shall be taken account of in considering whether the governor has failed to attend meetings of the governing body for a continuous period of six months for the purposes of sub-paragraph (2).

(5) A foundation governor, LEA governor, representative governor, partnership governor or co-opted governor who has been disqualified as a governor of a school under sub-paragraph (2) shall not be qualified for nomination or appointment as a governor of the same category at that school during the 12 months immediately following his disqualification under sub paragraph (2).

Bankruptcy

5 A person shall be disqualified for holding or continuing to hold office as a governor of a school if:

(1) he has been adjudged bankrupt or sequestration of his estate has been awarded and (in either case) he has not been discharged and the bankruptcy order has not been annulled or rescinded;

(2) he has made a composition or arrangement with, or granted a trust deed for, his creditors and has not been discharged in respect of it.

Disqualification of company directors

6 A person shall be disqualified for holding or for continuing to hold office as a governor of a school at any time when he is subject to a disqualification order under the Company Directors Disqualification Act 1 986**(a)** or to an order made under Section 429(2)(b) of the Insolvency Act 1986**(b)** (failure to pay under county court administration order).

Disqualification of charity trustees

7 A person shall be disqualified for holding or for continuing to hold office as a governor of a school if:

(1) he has been removed from the office of charity trustee or trustee for a charity by an order made by the Charity Commissioners or the High Court on the grounds of any misconduct or mismanagement in the administration of the charity for which he was responsible or to which he was privy, or which he by his conduct contributed to or facilitated; or

(2) he has been removed, under Section 7 of the Law Reform (Miscellaneous Provisions) (Scotland) Act 1990**(c)** (powers of Court of Session to deal with management of charities), from being concerned in the management or control of any body.

Persons whose employment is prohibited or restricted

8 (1) A person shall be disqualified for holding or for continuing to hold office as a governor of a school at any time when he is included in the list of teachers and workers with children or young persons whose employment is prohibited or restricted.

(2) In sub-paragraph (1), 'the list' means the list kept for the purposes of regulations made under Section 218(6) of the Education Reform Act 1988**(d)**.

(a) 1986 c 46.
(b) 1986 c 45.
(c) 1990 c 40.
(d) 1988 c 40. Section 218 of the 1998 Act has been amended by paragraph 17 of Schedule 30 to the 1998 Act.

Persons disqualified for being proprietors of independent schools

9   A person shall be disqualified for holding or continuing to hold office as a governor of a school at any time when he is, by virtue of an order made under Section 470 or Section 471 of the 1996 Act, disqualified for being the proprietor of any independent school or for being a teacher or other employee in any school.

Criminal convictions

10   (1)   Subject to sub-paragraph (6) below, a person shall be disqualified for holding, or for continuing to hold, office as a governor of a school where any of sub-paragraphs (3) to (5) or (7) below apply to him.

       (2)   In cases where a member of a governing body has continued in office as a governor of a school on transition to the new framework, in this paragraph, a reference to a person's appointment or election as governor, or becoming a governor *ex officio*, is a reference to his original appointment or election as a governor, or becoming a governor *ex officio*, within the terms of the 1996 Act.

       (3)   This sub-paragraph applies to a person if:

           (a)   within the period of five years ending with the date immediately preceding the date on which his appointment or election as governor would otherwise have taken effect or, as the case may be, on which he would otherwise have become a governor *ex officio*; or

           (b)   since his appointment or election as governor or, as the case may be, since he became a governor *ex officio*,

       he has been convicted, whether in the United Kingdom or elsewhere, of any offence and has had passed on him a sentence of imprisonment (whether suspended or not) for a period of not less than three months without the option of a fine.

       (4)   This sub-paragraph applies to a person if within the period of 20 years ending with the date immediately preceding the date on which his appointment or election as governor would otherwise have taken effect or, as the case may be, on which he would otherwise have become a governor *ex officio*, he has been convicted as aforesaid of any offence and has had passed on him a sentence of imprisonment for a period of not less than two and a half years.

       (5)   This sub-paragraph applies to a person if he has at any time been convicted as aforesaid of any offence and he has had passed on him a sentence of imprisonment for a period of not less than five years.

       (6)   For the purposes of sub-paragraphs (3) to (5) above, there shall be disregarded any conviction by or before a court outside the United Kingdom of an offence which, if the facts giving rise to the offence had taken place in any part of the United Kingdom, would not have constituted an offence under the law in force in that part of the United Kingdom.

       (7)   This sub-paragraph applies to a person if:

           (a)   within the period of five years ending with the date immediately preceding the date on which his appointment or election as governor would otherwise have taken effect or, as the case may be, on which he would otherwise have become a governor *ex officio*; or

           (b)   since his appointment or election as governor or, as the case may be, since he became a governor *ex officio*,

       he has been convicted under Section 547 of the 1996 Act (nuisance and disturbance on education premises) of an offence which took place on the premises of a school maintained by a local education authority or a grant-maintained school, and has been sentenced to a fine.

Notification to clerk

11   Where, by virtue of any paragraphs 5 to 10:

       (a)   a person becomes disqualified for holding, or for continuing to hold, office as a governor of a school; and

       (b)   he is, or is proposed, to become such a governor,

       he shall upon becoming so disqualified give written notice of that fact to the clerk to the governing body of the school.

Co-opted governor

12　A person shall be disqualified for appointment as a co-opted governor of a school other than an additional co-opted governor if he is:

(a)　a registered pupil at the school;

(b)　eligible to be a staff governor or a teacher governor of the school; or

(c)　an elected member of the local education authority.

Parent governor

13　A person shall be disqualified for appointment**(a)** as a parent governor of a school if he is:

(a)　an elected member of the local education authority,

(b)　an employee of the local education authority; or

(c)　an employee of the governing body of any school maintained by the local education authority;

unless he is a parent of a registered pupil at the school.

14　A person shall not be disqualified for continuing to hold office as a parent governor when he ceases to be a parent of a registered pupil at the school or to fulfil any of the requirements set out in paragraphs 5 or 6 of Schedule 2.

Partnership governors

15　A person shall be disqualified for nomination or appointment as a partnership governor of a school if he is:

(a)　a parent of a registered pupil at the school;

(b)　eligible to be a staff governor or a teacher governor of the school; or

(c)　an elected member or employee of the local education authority.

Teacher and staff governors

16　A teacher governor or a staff governor of a school shall, upon ceasing to be employed to work at the school, be disqualified for continuing to hold office as such a governor.

SCHEDULE 6

Regulation 57

RESTRICTIONS ON PERSONS TAKING PART IN PROCEEDINGS OF THE GOVERNING BODY OR THEIR COMMITTEES

Interpretation

1　(1)　In this Schedule, any reference, however expressed:

(a)　to a meeting of a school is a reference to a meeting of the governing body, or a committee of the governing body of a school;

(b)　to a relevant person present at a meeting of a school, so far as it concerns voting, is a reference only:

(i)　in the case of a meeting of the governing body, to a member of the governing body so present; and

(ii)　in the case of a meeting of a committee, to a member of the committee who is entitled to vote;

(c)　to a person's spouse includes someone living with that person as if he or she were that person's spouse.

Pecuniary interests

2　(1)　Subject to sub-paragraphs (5), (6) and (7), if a relevant person has any pecuniary interest, direct or indirect, in any contract, proposed contract or other matter and is present at a meeting of a school at which the contract or other matter is the subject of consideration, he shall at the meeting, and as soon a practicable after its commencement, disclose that

---

(a)　This paragraph does not apply to elected parent governors.

fact and withdraw from the meeting during the consideration or discussion of the contract or matter and he shall not vote on any question with respect to the contract or matter.

(2)   Subject to this paragraph, a governor of a school or any member of a committee of the governing body of a school may enter into a contract with the governing body of that school from which he is entitled to profit.

(3)   For the purposes of this paragraph, a person shall be treated as having an indirect pecuniary interest in a contract, proposed contract or other matter if:

(a)   he or any nominee of his is a member, or he is an employee, of a corporation or other body with which the contract was made or is proposed to be made or which has a direct pecuniary interest in the matter under consideration, or

(b)   he is a partner, or is in the employment, of a person with whom the contract was made or is proposed to be made or who has a direct pecuniary interest in the matter under consideration:

provided that a person shall not by virtue of this sub-paragraph be treated as having such an interest by reason only of his membership of, or employment by, any public body; or by reason of his membership of a corporation or other body if he has no financial interest in any securities of that corporation or other body.

(4)   For the purposes of this paragraph, a person shall be treated as having a direct or indirect pecuniary interest in a contract, proposed contract or other matter if a relative (including his spouse) living with him, to his knowledge has, or would be treated as having, such an interest, direct or indirect.

(5)   For the purposes of this paragraph, a member of the governing body or of a committee of the governing body of a school who is a person employed to work at the school as a teacher, or the headteacher, whether he is a governor or not, shall not be treated as having a direct or indirect pecuniary interest in a contract, proposed contract or other matter by reason only:

(a)   of having an interest in the contract or matter which is no greater than the interest of the generality of teachers employed to work at the school;

(b)   of the fact that the contract or matter under consideration or discussion concerns the exercise by the governing body of any of their functions relating to the curriculum for the school; or

(c)   of the fact that the contract or matter under consideration or discussion involves expenditure by the governing body.

(6)   For the purposes of this paragraph, a member of the governing body or of a committee of the governing body of a school who is a person employed to work at the school otherwise than as a teacher, shall not be treated as having a direct or indirect pecuniary interest in a contract, proposed contract or other matter by reason only:

(a)   of having an interest in the contract or matter which is no greater than the interest of the generality of persons employed to work at the school otherwise than as teachers;

(b)   of the fact that the contract or matter under consideration or discussion concerns the exercise by the governing body of any of their functions relating to the curriculum for the school; or

(c)   of the fact that the contract or matter under consideration or discussion involves expenditure by the governing body.

(7)   Members of the governing body shall not, by reason of their pecuniary interest in the matter, be prevented from considering and voting upon proposals for the governing body to take out insurance protecting its members against liabilities incurred by them arising out of their office and the governing body shall not, by reason of the pecuniary interest of its members, be prevented from obtaining such insurance and paying the premiums.

(8)   In this paragraph, 'securities' shall be interpreted in accordance with Section 142 of the Financial Services Act 1986**(a)**.

(a)   1986 c 60.

Office of governor, chairman or clerk

3   (1)   This sub-paragraph applies where a relevant person is present at a meeting of the school at which a subject of consideration is:

   (a)   his own appointment, reappointment or removal as a member of the governing body or a committee of the governing body;

   (b)   his own appointment or removal from office as clerk to or chairman or vice-chairman of the governing body or clerk to or chairman of a committee of the governing body; or

   (c)   if he is an additional co-opted governor nominated by a particular category of person, any determination under paragraph 15(1) of Schedule 9 to the 1998 Act as to the provision in the instrument of government for additional co-opted governors nominated by that category of person.

   (2)   In any case where sub-paragraph (1) applies, the relevant person shall withdraw from the meeting during the consideration or discussion of the matter in question and shall not vote on any question with respect to that matter.

Pay or appraisal of persons working at the school

4   (1)   This sub-paragraph applies where a relevant person who is employed to work at a school other than as headteacher is present at a meeting of the school at which a subject of consideration is the pay or performance appraisal of any particular person employed to work at the school.

   (2)   This sub-paragraph applies where a headteacher of a school is present at a meeting of the school at which a subject of consideration is his own pay or performance appraisal.

   (3)   In any case where sub-paragraph (1) or (2) applies, the person first-mentioned in that sub-paragraph shall withdraw from the meeting during the consideration or discussion of the matter in question and shall not vote on any question with respect to that matter.

SCHEDULE 7

Regulation 58

TRANSITIONAL PROVISIONS

Qualifications and disqualifications

1   Regulation 15 and Schedule 5 shall apply in relation to any member of a transitional governing body constituted under an instrument of government in accordance with Regulation 18(2) of the First Transitional Regulations but shall not apply in relation to any member of:

   (a)   a transitional governing body constituted under Regulation 19 of the First Transitional Regulations; or

   (b)   a transitional governing body, a GM transitional governing body, or a grouped transitional governing body within the meaning of the Second Transitional Regulations**(a)**.

2   In relation to England, Regulation 23 of and Schedule 6 to the First Transitional Regulations, and Regulations 21, 40 and 53 of, and Schedule 6 to the Second Transitional Regulations, are revoked.

3   (1)   In relation to England, for Regulation 13(10) of the First Transitional Regulations there is substituted the following paragraph:

   '(10)   This regulation is subject to Regulation 14 (surplus governors) and paragraphs 1 to 11, 14 and 16 of Schedule 5 to the Education (School Government) (England) Regulations 1999 (qualifications and disqualifications).'.

   (2)   In relation to England, for Regulation 33(8) of the Second Transitional Regulations there is substituted the following paragraph:

   '(8)   This regulation is subject to Regulation 34 (surplus governors) and paragraphs 1 to 11, 14 and 16 of Schedule 5 to the Education (School Government) (England) Regulations 1999 (qualifications and disqualifications).'.

(a)   The First Transitional Regulations and the Second Transitional Regulations provide for disqualification requirements in relation to members of the transitional governing bodies specified in paragraph l(a) and (b) of Schedule 7 to follow disqualification requirements under the 1996 Act.

Term of office

4   (1)   A governor who continues as a governor of a school (other than as headteacher or as an *ex officio* foundation governor) pursuant to Regulation 13 of the First Transitional Regulations, Regulation 13 of the First Transitional Regulations as it applies by virtue of Regulation 20 of those Regulations, or Regulation 33 of the Second Transitional Regulations, shall hold office for the remainder of the term for which he was originally appointed or elected, but for no longer than four years from 1 September 1999.

       (2)   A governor appointed by the local education authority under Regulation 19(4) of the First Transitional Regulations or Regulation 30(4) of the Second Transitional Regulations shall hold office for a term of four years.

       (3)   In relation to England, for Regulation 57(7) of the Second Transitional Regulations there shall be substituted the following paragraph:

          '(7)   Subject to paragraph (6), any governor to whom this regulation applies, other than a governor appointed by the Secretary of State under Section 18 of the 1998 Act, shall hold office for the remainder of the term for which he was appointed, but for no longer than four years from the appointed day.'.

5   Any co-opted governor (other than an additional co-opted governor) appointed for the purposes of the constitution or reconstitution of the governing body and referred to in Regulations 14(3), 35(1) or 47(3) of the Second Transitional Regulations shall hold office for the term of one year.

6   In relation to England, the following Regulations are revoked:

       (a)   Regulation 22 of the First Transitional Regulations;

       (b)   Regulations 20, 39 and 52 of the Second Transitional Regulations.

Removal

7   (1)   For the purposes of Regulation 18(1), any initial foundation governor (within the meaning of the 1996 Act) on the transitional governing body of a former grant-maintained school under Regulation 19 of the First Transitional Regulations shall be treated as having been appointed by the person or persons entitled immediately before 1 September 1999 to appoint foundation governors under provision included in the instrument of government (in accordance with Section 228(7)(b) of the 1996 Act).

       (2)   The power of removal in Regulation 18(1) does not apply in respect of:

       (a)   a first governor within the meaning of the 1996 Act; or

       (b)   a parent governor within the meaning of the 1996 Act who has been appointed rather than elected.

       (3)   The power of removal in Regulation 18(4) does not apply in respect of any co-opted governor on transition to the new schools framework under the 1998 Act unless the governing body conducting the school is constituted or partly constituted under the instrument of government.

Clerks and chairman at new schools on transition to the new framework

8   (1)   This paragraph applies in relation to a school or proposed school:

       (a)   to which Regulation 13 of the School Organisation Regulations applies; or

       (b)   to which Regulation 13 of the Second Transitional Regulations applies.

       (2)   In this paragraph, 'transitional governing body' has the meaning in the Second Transitional Regulations.

       (3)   Where this paragraph applies, the person who on 31 August 1999 was the clerk to or the chairman or vice-chairman of the temporary governing body (within the meaning of the 1996 Act) shall continue in office from 1 September 1999 on the temporary governing body or transitional governing body, as the case may be.

       (4)   Subject to sub-paragraph (3), provisions in Part IV relating to the clerk to the temporary governing body, and provisions in Regulation 31 relating to the chairman and vice-chairman of the temporary governing body, shall apply in relation to the clerk, chairman and vice-chairman (as the case may be) of any school to which this paragraph applies.

Clerks at degrouping schools

9 (1) In this regulation 'grouped school' means any school treated for the purposes of the Second Transitional Regulations as a school grouped under Section 89 or 280 of the Education Act 1996 immediately before 1 September 1999 and 'grouped governing body' means the governing body of such a school as constituted under the 1996 Act or Regulation 49 of the Second Transitional Regulations, as the case may be.

(2) The person who was the clerk to the grouped governing body shall act as clerk to each governing body constituted under an instrument of government who succeed them in accordance with the Second Transitional Regulations, pending the appointment of each such governing body's clerk.

Amendment of the First and Second Transitional Regulations in relation to co-opted governors

10 (1) In relation to England, the First Transitional Regulations are amended:

(a) by the omission of Regulation 16(3) and the omission of the word 'additional' in Regulation 16(4);

(b) by the omission of Schedule 3 to those Regulations.

(2) In relation to England, the Second Transitional Regulations are amended:

(a) by the omission of Regulation 16(2) and the omission of the word 'additional' in Regulation 16(3);

(b) by the omission of Regulation 36(3) and the omission of the word 'additional' in Regulation 36(4);

(c) by the omission of Schedule 3.

Miscellaneous

11 In relation to England, in Regulation 42(2)(b) of the Second Transitional Regulations after 'paragraph 4 or 9 of' there shall be inserted 'Schedule 6 to'.

EXPLANATORY NOTE

(This note is not part of the Regulations)

These Regulations deal with the government of maintained schools and new schools in England, from 1 September 1999, when the new framework for schools under the School Standards and Framework Act 1998 comes into effect. They work together with Schedules 9 to 12 to that Act.

Part I provides for the regulations to come into force generally on 1 September 1999. Restrictions on who can be appointed as clerk to the governing body or to certain committees, and new procedures for the appointment of the chairman and vice-chairman of the governing body, come into force on 1 April 2000. Part I also contains interpretation provisions. In particular, the general principle is that references in the regulations to governing bodies include temporary governing bodies of new schools.

The making of new instruments of government for maintained schools on transition to the new framework, and the constitution or reconstitution of governing bodies under those instruments, is dealt with in separate regulations under Schedules 9 to 12 to the 1998 Act. Part II of the Regulations makes provision for copies of the new instruments of government to be provided to governing bodies and to the other parties involved in making the instrument of government.

The rest of Part II applies to maintained schools which have new framework governing bodies constituted under instruments of government. It relates to provisions which may be in the instrument, having regard to the fact that the instrument may be amended in accordance with Schedule 12 to the 1998 Act after it has been made. Regulation 6 and Schedule 1 relate to provision in instruments of government for additional co-opted governors nominated by sponsors or an Education Action Forum. Regulation 7 requires the instrument of government to be amended if there is any change in the body entitled to appoint a representative governor at a community special school. Regulation 8 requires the instrument of government to provide for appointment of a substitute foundation governor if an *ex officio* foundation governor cannot or will not act.

Part II also deals with appointments and elections of governors at schools which have new framework governing bodies constituted under instruments of government. Regulation 9 and Schedules 2 and 3 provide for new appointments of parent and partnership governors. Regulation 10 provides for notification of vacancies and appointments. Regulation 11 provides for appointments to be made in accordance with a direction given by the Secretary of State where joint appointors cannot agree. Regulation 12 and Schedule 4 provide for the election of governors. Regulation 13 provides for the removal of surplus governors where there are more governors of a particular type than are required by the instrument.

Part III makes provision for qualifications and disqualifications for office, term of office and resignation and removal of governors, other than temporary governors of new schools.

Regulation 15 and Schedule 5 set out disqualification provisions relating to governors, imposing a number of new disqualifications. These provisions apply to all governing bodies, except temporary governing bodies and governing bodies, which (for a short period on transition to the new framework) continue as constituted under the 1996 Act provisions by virtue of Regulations under Schedule 10 to the 1998 Act.

Regulation 16 provides that generally governors hold office for four years. The main exceptions are for governors continuing in office on transition to the new framework, the first co-opted governors at new schools, and foundation governors appointed on or after 1 September 1999.

Regulation 17 provides that any governor can at any time resign. Regulations 18 and 19 contain new provisions about the removal of governors. Regulation 20 requires notice of resignation or removal.

Part IV provides for the appointment of clerks to governing bodies and temporary governing bodies. Clerks at community, voluntary-controlled or community special schools are appointed and dismissed by the local education authority as directed by the governing body. Clerks at foundation, voluntary-aided, or foundation special schools are appointed and dismissed by the governing body. Special provisions apply where the school does not have a delegated budget and in respect of the appointment of the first clerk to a temporary governing body.

Part V provides for meetings and proceedings of governing bodies and temporary governing bodies. This Part includes provision for appointment and removal of the chairman, convening and termination of meetings, quorum, decisions to be made by the majority of members voting, access to meetings, minutes and their publication. Regulations 41-44 relate to delegation of governing body functions.

Part VI deals with committees of governing bodies and temporary governing bodies. It covers establishment and constitution of committees (including staff dismissal, dismissal appeal, pupil discipline and admissions committees), disqualifications for office as a member of a committee of any person who is not a governor of the school, clerking of committees, proceedings, minutes and access to meetings of committees.

Part VII and Schedule 6 contain new provisions relating to withdrawal from governing body or committee meetings of persons normally entitled to attend those meetings. The general principle is that where there is a conflict between the interests of such a person and the interests of the governing body, or where the principles of natural justice require a fair hearing and there is any reasonable doubt about the person's ability to act impartially, he should withdraw from the meeting and not vote.

Part VIII and Schedule 7 contain transitional provisions.

APPENDIX C: THE HOUSE OF COMMONS EDUCATION AND EMPLOYMENT COMMITTEE INQUIRY REPORT: 'THE ROLE OF SCHOOL GOVERNORS' JULY 1999

SUMMARY OF CONCLUSIONS AND RECOMMENDATIONS

Introduction

1 School governors are a large, usually unsung, army of volunteers whose contribution to the life of our schools has been too little appreciated (paragraph 1).

The governing body and the local community

2 We agree with the many witnesses who highlighted the important role that governing bodies play in ensuring a direct line of accountability from the school to its local community (paragraph 10).

Raising standards

3 We support the Government's emphasis that the governing body's main purpose should be helping to raise standards of achievement (paragraph 12).

4 We recommend that governing bodies agree and publish the criteria on which they judge their school's success. Such criteria would include the results of public examinations such as SATs or GCSEs, but should not be limited to narrowly-defined academic achievements. Other measures of pupils' success, in areas such as music, drama and sport, all play a vital part in the life of any school, as does the development of successful links with parents and the local community. Identifying such criteria will help ensure that the governing body can focus on the really important activities of the school, rather than just the day-to-day problems of managing a complex organisation (paragraph 12).

5 We see great merit in all governing bodies devoting, on at least an annual basis, one meeting to a formal review of standards of achievement in their school. This would complement what we expect should be a continuous process of monitoring throughout the school year. It should certainly not be the only occasion on which standards are considered. Indeed, it might well be appropriate for every full governors' meeting to have 'standards of achievement' as an agenda item. The annual review meeting would include consideration of the relevant comparative performance data for the school, including the school's performance and assessment (PANDA) report supplied by OFSTED, a report from the headteacher, information on SATs and other examination results and any other information which the LEA provides (paragraph 13).

6 Information designed to help governors assess pupils' achievement must always be available in a format which governors, who are volunteers, often pressed for time, can easily digest. Such information should not be couched in educational jargon or 'teacher-speak' (paragraph 13).

'Governance' skills

7 We believe that the governing body's responsibilities extend beyond representing the school's local community, but this does not mean that the governing body should be assembled simply to provide a range of professional skills for the school (paragraph 14).

8 We agree that relying too heavily on the professional skills of individual governors may run the danger of distorting the proper role of the governing body. We therefor emphasise that the priority for governing bodies is to ensure they are able to exercise effective **governance** skills (paragraph 16).

9 We conclude that although schools in disadvantaged areas may not always be able to draw their governors from the 'professional classes', it would be patronising to assume that they will automatically suffer as a result. Nevertheless, schools in such areas often face the most difficult challenges, and will benefit from working with the most effective governing bodies (paragraph 17).

Clarifying the governing body's role

10 We accept that the role of governing bodies is well-defined in law. Nevertheless, we believe that greater effort needs to be made to ensure that all governors have a clear understanding of their role. High-quality guidance should be made available which provides an interpretation of their statutory role in a form suitable for all governors. We believe that the analogy with the role of non-executive directors is helpful (paragraph 19).

11 Although national terms of reference for governing bodies will set an important framework for the way in which governors carry out their work, it will remain the case that different divisions of labour between governing bodies and the school's management will suit schools in differing circumstances. Governors and headteachers must retain the flexibility to work out the best way to fulfil their responsibilities to the school (paragraph 19).

Membership of governing bodies

12 We believe that it is a key responsibility for LEAs to support their schools by nominating only individuals with a commitment to education to serve as governors. We welcome the increase in the number of LEAs which are opening up their governor appointment processes. We believe that the important point is to ensure that the method by which LEA governors are appointed is transparent. Therefor, we recommend that all LEAs publish the criteria on which they select individuals to be nominated to serve on governing bodies. We do not believe that simply being active in local party politics should be the determining factor in such nominations. Commitment to education, a desire to

support the school concerned and a willingness to serve the local community should be at the heart of any such criteria (paragraph 27).

13 LEAs should also ensure that vacancies among LEA-appointed governors are filled promptly (paragraph 27).

14 We recommend that all LEAs collect information on the vacancy rates of each governor category in their area and make this information publicly-available (paragraph 29).

Barriers to governor recruitment

15 On balance, we do not believe it would be practical to require all employers to provide a minimum amount of paid time off for employees to undertake their work as school governors (paragraph 35).

16 However, if paid time off work remains a significant barrier to recruitment we believe the DfEE should reconsider whether chairs of governing bodies, at least, should be entitled to some paid time off (paragraph 36).

17 We understand the natural reluctance of governing bodies to use funding which might otherwise be available to spend directly on pupils at their school. However, to be effective and representative, governing bodies need to be able to recruit and retain the right people, from all sections of the local community. Governing bodies – and others – need to recognise that spending money on governors' expenses can be a proper use of school funds if it helps ensure that governing bodies can work effectively. We agree with the DfEE that it would be inappropriate to ring-fence money for this purpose within the school's budget. But the DfEE should ensure that the total level of resources available to schools includes sufficient funds to meet the legitimate expenses of governing bodies (paragraph 40).

18 It would be helpful for the DfEE to also give more detailed indicative guidance about what could be regarded as reasonable levels of expenses. LEAs, working with local associations, might also wish to draw up locally-specific guidance on this subject which would reflect specific local conditions (paragraph 40).

Recruitment strategies

19 We welcome the Government's proposal to develop 'one stop shops' for governor recruitment in the six Excellence in Cities areas. However, we believe there would be value in extending the scope of these 'one stop shops' to include all categories of governor recruitment, not just co-opted governors. If 'one stop shops' are to be part of the solution to recruitment difficulties, acting as a brokerage service, it is important that they maintain lists of all potential governors, as well as all governor vacancies. One stop shops could then be in a position to suggest names of potential LEA governors, as well as raising awareness of the importance of parent governors. One stop shops could also support other organisations in their drive to recruit governors. Encouragement could be given to those people who expressed an interest in some form of public service, and the one stop shop could provide general information about the work of governing bodies as well as specific information about governor vacancies. The DfEE and local authorities

should take an imaginative approach to the creation of one stop shops – they could have outlets in community centres, health centres or supermarkets, and they could be backed up by telephone or Internet facilities (paragraph 42).

20 We recommend that a clear, targeted strategy is developed to ensure schools in disadvantaged areas are provided with appropriate support to ensure they can recruit sufficient governors from their local community (paragraph 44).

21 We recommend that LEA organisations, such as the Local Government Association (LGA), working with the national governor associations, establish a forum to exchange good practice on recruitment strategies to target specific communities and localities (paragraph 44).

22 The DfEE and NGC ethnic minority recruitment initiative should consider including support for translation services for governors, where this is required, to ensure that governing bodies fully represent the local community (paragraph 46).

23 We see value in considering recruiting from 'non-traditional' sources such as students on initial teacher training (ITT) programmes or undergraduate students (paragraph 47).

Removing governors

24 We welcome the Government's commitment to end the option of reappointing LEA governors who have been removed from a governing body due to non-attendance (paragraph 48).

25 We believe that cases of 'rogue' governors are relatively infrequent. However, we recognise the significant detrimental effect that 'rogue' governors can have on a governing body and its school. The key characteristic of the 'rogue' governor is that he or she acts in a manner that disregards the corporate nature and responsibilities of the governing body We therefor consider that, in extreme cases where the relationship between an individual governor and the majority of the governing body has irretrievably broken down, there should be mechanisms to remove governors from the governing body, and that these should apply to all categories of governor (paragraph 50).

26 We recommend that proceedings to remove individual governors, apart from reasons of non-attendance, should be restricted to clearly-defined cases. Later in our report we recommend that governing bodies adopt a code of practice covering the relations between the head and governors, governors' conduct in the school, etc. Only in cases where there has been a clear breach of this code of practice would we recommend that procedures to remove a governor be invoked. We recommend that the DfEE bring forward proposals to allow all categories of governor to be removed from office. We would expect that such an action would require at least two-thirds of those eligible to vote to support a resolution removing the governor from office. Any mechanism would have to take account of the principles of natural justice (paragraph 50).

Pupil representation

27 We welcome the existence of School Councils, and wish to see all schools establish such bodies. We recommend that governing bodies establish consultative arrangements to

ensure governors are aware of pupils' opinions. Such arrangements should include opportunities for pupils to make presentations to the governing body, or for a governor to attend, by invitation, meetings of the School Council (paragraph 51).

Workload

28 We conclude that, properly managed, the workload of governors is not too burdensome (paragraph 55).

29 We believe that governors' workload could be better managed through improved information flow to governors, more opportunities for sharing best practice and networking and better management of governing body business. The restatement, by Government and others, of the role of governing bodies would also help (paragraph 55).

30 Official documents should, as a matter of routine, include a summary and should highlight points for action or consideration by the recipient (paragraph 58).

31 We recommend that the DfEE establish a task force to improve the quality and reduce the quantity of paperwork that governors receive. This should consider the duplication of information from LEA and government sources and take the relatively simple step of ensuring paperwork is produced in a common, user-friendly format, with appropriate cross-referencing to other relevant documents. As is customary with many other documents, key points for action or consideration, plus a summary of the document, should be a standard part of all documents for governors. We repeat that papers aimed at an audience of governors should eschew educational jargon and 'teacher-speak' (paragraph 58).

The respective roles of the governing body and the headteacher

32 The relationship between heads and governing bodies is crucial. A clear statement of the respective roles the Government expects them to play in the forthcoming terms of reference will be welcome, although (as we noted earlier) it will perhaps not be desirable to try and set these down in tablets of stone. Our priority is to ensure that governing bodies discharge their duties effectively. It is not in the interest of pupils for the headteacher to 'manage' the governing body, or for the governing body to interfere in the proper duties of the headteacher. We therefor recommend that governing bodies and headteachers in each school agree how their respective roles should be fulfilled. Such an agreement could form a part of the code of practice for governing bodies (paragraph 61).

Governors' work in schools

33 We agree with the Government that governors do not have a role in 'inspecting' work in the classroom. It is the responsibility of the governing body to monitor standards of achievement, to be accountable for them and to ensure that weaknesses are addressed. However, it is not helpful for individual governors to us this responsibility as the basis for inspecting individual teachers (paragraph 62).

A code of practice for governing bodies

34 We recommend that governing bodies adopt a code of practice outlining the purpose of the governing body which sets out what all parties agree is the appropriate relationship between individual governors, the whole governing body and the school. It would also cover appropriate conduct of governors in the school. We recommend that the DfEE take a lead in developing a model code of practice, after consultation with governors' organisations, headteacher associations, LEAs and other bodies as appropriate (paragraph 64).

Governors' work with parents and the local community

35 We recommend that the statutory requirement for the governing body to hold an annual meeting with parents be ended, although the requirement to produce an annual report should remain. Governing bodies will need to consider alternative ways in which to communicate effectively with the school's parents, and how best to provide opportunities for parents to discuss issues with the governing body (paragraph 66).

Headteacher appraisal and pay determination

36 It is too early to comment on how well governing bodies will be able to discharge the responsibility for performance management proposed in the Green Paper. We may wish to return to this issue when governing bodies have had some experience of managing these new arrangements. Nevertheless, we recognise governors' and headteachers' concerns. If the Government's proposals are to be introduced successfully, governing bodies need to be supported to ensure they have the confidence to operate the new scheme. For a start, the DfEE should produce as soon as possible both Part One and Part Two of the Performance Management Handbook. We welcome the Government's commitment to provide training and external advice to prepare and support governing bodies for their role in performance management. But it will be essential for governors to take up this training and to spend the money which the Government is to allocate for it. Elsewhere we consider networking arrangements to allow governors to share ideas and good practice. We believe that governors will benefit greatly from opportunities to exchange views on performance management (paragraph 72).

Local education authorities' support for governors

37 We commend those LEAs who are providing high-quality support and training for their governing bodies. However, more must be done to spread this good practice. We recommend that the Government, working with the Local Government Association, the national and local governors' associations, and the National Co-ordinators of Governors' Services group initiate schemes to spread the best practice in providing support for governors. Issues such as the provision of high-quality training, encouraging governors' forums and creating mechanisms to keep governors up-to-date with education developments are all important considerations for LEAs. Support for governing bodies is an important part of LEAs' contribution to school improvement. Therefor we

recommend that OFSTED's inspection of LEAs includes discussion with governors, for example, through organising a meeting with the local governors' forum, where one exists, to gather views on the effectiveness of the LEA's support for the governing body (paragraph 75).

38 We recommend that LEAs ensure that governing bodies and individual governors can contact their school's attached adviser directly in order to obtain information on the school's performance (paragraph 76).

Training and induction

39 Some examples of nationally-validated training for school governors exist, for example, the BTEC award in school governorship developed by Essex County Council. This is a welcome development. We recommend that the DfEE give consideration to developing a scheme to provide quality assurance for governor training, perhaps by way of national accreditation. We note the importance of high-quality training for governors, and in particular the value of whole governing body training and joint training of the governing body and the headteacher (paragraph 78).

40 We do not believe that training for governors and chairs of governing bodies should be mandatory except in the case of induction training: see recommendation 41 (paragraph 80).

41 We recognise the importance of induction training for new governors and newly appointed chairs of governing bodies. Evidence has shown that high-quality induction is critical to enabling governors to make an effective contribution to the work of their governing body. We therefor recommend that induction training be made a **requirement** of all governors when first appointed, and for newly-appointed chairs of governors. We believe that joint training for new chairs of governing bodies and their headteacher will be particularly valuable. We recognise the concerns put to us that a requirement to undergo training may act as a barrier to recruitment of governors. However, we firmly believe that governors have an important role to play in improving schools. It is therefor important that they are given at least a basic introduction to their responsibilities and how best to discharge them (paragraph 82).

42 We firmly believe that money targeted at improving the effectiveness of the governing body will do much to improve the effectiveness of the school as a whole. We therefor urge governing bodies to use the discretion they have in the Standards Fund to identify training opportunities which will improve their own effectiveness. Nevertheless, we recognise that some governing bodies will find it difficult to justify expenditure on training or support for themselves when there are many other calls on their school's budget. We therefor recommend that the DfEE, working in partnership with the national associations, publicise examples of good practice where expenditure on governing body training or professional support has made a significant contribution to school improvement (paragraph 83).

43 We believe that training for new headteachers on working effectively with governing bodies and chairs of governors should be available for newly-appointed headteachers.

Although we do not recommend that this is a requirement, it would be in the best interests of individual governing bodies to require such training as part of the appraisal process for their newly-appointed headteacher (paragraph 84).

Other sources of support

44 We recommend that the National Association of Governors and Managers, the National Governors' Council and Information for School and College Governors consider ways in which they can work together in partnership. For instance, they could develop a single point of contact for the range of 'advice line' services they run. These services could be 're-launched' and promoted widely as a national source of independent, expert advice. Such an initiative would allow for more cost-effective funding and support from the DfEE (paragraph 85).

45 Where they do not already exist, we recommend the establishment of local governor associations or governors' forums to provide opportunities for governors to share best practice and discuss common issues (paragraph 86).

46 We recommend that Government provide support for local governor forums, either through the voluntary associations or via LEAs (paragraph 86).

47 We recommend that all LEAs establish a pool of experienced governors who are willing to work with governing bodies which request support and advice on particular issues. Schools which face severe challenges or experience difficulty in recruiting governors may wish to draw on the services of other experienced governors within the LEA. Such governors would complement governors drawn from the local community rather than replace them, and therefor would not automatically join the governing body. Instead, they would work alongside the school's governors, perhaps in a mentoring role or offering particular support to the chairs of governing bodies (paragraph 87).

Role of the clerk to the governing body

48 We agree with witnesses who argued that effective clerking services made a significant contribution to the work of effective governing bodies. We believe the cost of such services is a worthwhile investment for governing bodies, and we hope that all governing bodies will use such services. We recommend that all LEAs should offer clerking services to their schools, although schools should not be obliged to subscribe to services from their LEA. Information should be widely-available from all providers of clerking and other governor support and training services, including other LEAs and further education colleges, so that governing bodies have a choice of provider (paragraph 88).

Recognising governors' contribution

49 We recommend that all LEAs consider ways of acknowledging the contribution made by effective, long-serving governors to education in their community (paragraph 89).

50 On taking up a post as a school governor, we recommend that governors receive a letter from the Secretary of State thanking them for their service to the community and underlining the importance of their role (paragraph 90).

Recognising governors' employers

51 We recommend that **employers** of newly-appointed governors also receive a letter, perhaps from the Secretary of State. The letter would highlight the importance of school governorship and note the demands made on governors, especially the time required to make an effective contribution. The letter would also urge the employer to consider supporting their employee, particularly in terms of paid time off (paragraph 91).

52 In order to give public recognition to the contribution which employers make, we recommend that the Government establish a scheme which celebrates those organisations which provide high levels of support for their employees who serve as governors. Such support might include a guarantee of a minimum number of days off per year for governing body business. We recommend that this scheme be called the 'Investors in Education' awards (paragraph 92).

536162

on or before the last due ‚
˺ below .